The statue of Blaga at his birthplace, Lancrăm. Photo: R.T. Allen

Lucian Blaga

Selected philosophical extracts

Edited by
**Angela Botez,
R.T. Allen,
Henrieta Anișoara Șerban**

Vernon Series in Philosophy

Copyright © 2018 Vernon Press, an imprint of Vernon Art and Science Inc, on behalf of the author.

All rights reserved. No part of this publication may be reproduced, stored in a retrieval system, or transmitted in any form or by any means, electronic, mechanical, photocopying, recording, or otherwise, without the prior permission of Vernon Art and Science Inc.

www.vernonpress.com

In the Americas:
Vernon Press
1000 N West Street,
Suite 1200, Wilmington,
Delaware 19801
United States

In the rest of the world:
Vernon Press
C/Sancti Espiritu 17,
Malaga, 29006
Spain

Vernon Series in Philosophy

Library of Congress Control Number: 2017955749

ISBN: 978-1-62273-293-7

Product and company names mentioned in this work are the trademarks of their respective owners. While every care has been taken in preparing this work, neither the authors nor Vernon Art and Science Inc. may be held responsible for any loss or damage caused or alleged to be caused directly or indirectly by the information contained in it.

Cover image used with the permission of Mrs Dorli Blaga and the Foreign Languages Publishing House, Bucharest.

Table of Contents

Acknowledgements		*ix*
The Editors		*xi*
Foreword		*xvii*
Chapter 1	**Introduction: Life and Philosophy**	1
Chapter 2	**From *Philosophical self-presentation* (1938): A lecture delivered at the University of Cluj**	27
Chapter 3	**From *The Dogmatic Aeon* (1931)**	37
Chapter 4	**From *The Divine Differentials* (1940)**	45
Chapter 5	**From *Transcendental Censorship* (1934)**	63
Chapter 6	**From *Luciferian Knowledge* (1933)**	71
Chapter 7	**From *Science and Creation* (1942)**	83
Chapter 8	**From *The Genesis of Metaphor and the Meaning of Culture* (1937)**	97
Chapter 9	**From *Horizon and Style* (1935)**	105
Chapter 10	**From *The Mioritic Space* (1936)**	129
Chapter 11	**Aphorisms**	141
Glossary		*149*
Bibliography		*163*
Index		*177*

Acknowledgements

We would like to express our gratitude to all those who contributed to the release of this book, meant both for the Romanian and the foreign reader. First, to the Scientific Publishing House, and to its director Dinu Grama, who in 1996 published **Dimensiunea metafizică operei lui Lucian Blaga** (*The Metaphysical Dimension of Lucian Blaga's Works*), ed. Angela Botez. Then to the staff of the *Romanian Review* (which has ceased publication), within the Foreign Languages Press Group, which for many years embraced the proposal to present the Romanian philosopher, translating in languages of world circulation several philosophical texts, mainly from Blaga's creation, as well as interesting studies and commentaries on Blaga's work written between the wars and by contemporary critics. With the concern, dedication and skill of such editors—men of letters, philosophers, historians and aestheticians—such as Victor Botez, Valentin F. Mihăescu, Aurel Rău, Șerban Stati, Nicolae Sarambei, two issues and several special collections dedicated to Lucian Blaga have been published. There were over one thousand pages translated into English, French and German; therefore we feel it is our duty to express our thanks to the translators, to those people overcoming the difficulties of the texts and revealing to the world, beyond the borders of the Romanian language, the ideas and the outlooks of this outstanding contemporary philosopher: Andrei Bantaș, Ileana Barbu, Nicolae Barna, Georgeta Bolomey, Alina Carac, Angela Crocus, Agnes Davidovici, Eugen Gasnas, Hugo Hausl, Florin Ionescu, Adrian Ivana, Mihaela Mihăilaș, Cristina Niculescu, Delia Răzdolescu, Micaela Slăvescu, Anda Țeodorescu, Delia Ursulescu and Monica Voiculescu. Also, special thanks to Professor Calvin Schrag, Professor Eric Ramsey, and Dr Michael Jones for their commentaries, help and advice.

We would also like to give special thanks to Mrs Dorli Blaga (Lucian Blaga's daughter), one of the owners of the copyright, for their permission to publish this volume, and also to the former management of the *Romanian Review*, and of the *Revue roumaine de philosophie* (1995-2010) published at the Romanian Academy Publishing House, Editor-in-Chief Professor Angela Botez, PhD, for having allowed us to quote excerpts from issues dedicated to Lucian Blaga in the present volume, which, we hope, will make Blaga's philosophy better known in the English-speaking world.

We express our consideration as well to several researchers from the Department of Epistemology of the Institute of Philosophy and Psychology 'Constantin Rădulescu-Motru' of the Romanian Academy who contributed to the definitive form of this volume with suggestions for the structuring and restructuring of the volume and improved the outcome through adequate adjustments of the translations: Henrieta Anişoara Şerban, PhD, Bogdan Popescu, PhD, Oana Vasilescu, PhD, Marius Augustin Drăghici, PhD, and to Ms. Gabriela Petrescu and Ms. Jeana Marinache for the technical editing.

Angela Botez and R.T. Allen

The Editors

Professor Angela Botez is President of the Section of Philosophy, Psychology and Theology of the Academy of Romanian Scientists, and Full Member of the Academy of Romanian Scientists.

Dr Henrieta Anişoara Şerban is a Scientific Researcher at the Institute of Political Science and International Relations, 'Ion I. C. Brătianu', and at the Institute of Philosophy and Psychology, 'Constantin Rădulescu-Motru,' of the Romanian Academy, also a Corresponding Member of the Academy of Romanian Scientists.

Dr R.T. Allen is retired and was a Lecturer and Senior Lecturer in Philosophy of Education at Colleges in England and Nigeria and at The University of the West Indies, Trinidad.

Foreword

It has been said of Dostoevsky that he was Russia's greatest metaphysician. With equal propriety it can be said of Lucian Blaga that he was Romania's greatest metaphysician. His philosophical treatises and his poetry have played a prominent role in the constitution of Romania's distinctive cultural life and history. It should be noted, however, that Blaga's metaphysics, in many respects not unlike that of Dostoevsky, was of a personal and mundane- rooted sort. Although systematic in its analysis of metaphysical details, Blaga never aspired to fashion a closed, final, and fully elaborated system. Throughout his career he succumbed neither to the stratospheric planking of abstract categories that defined much of the metaphysics of the ancients nor to the overdetermination of alleged indubitable knowledge claims within the epistemology of the moderns.

The open-texture quality of Blaga's metaphysics and epistemology, always conjoined with an historicist grounding in the changing patterns of development, had profound effects upon the wider cultural complex as an interweaving of multi-disciplinary approaches to the issues that intrigue the human spirit. For an engagement with such multi-disciplinary endeavors Blaga was well suited. As a veritable polymath, versatile not only in his innovative metaphysics, he was also a published poet, a playwright, a novelist, and a frequent producer of essays. In addition, it is important to note that he was also learned in the physics and biology of his day and was thus able to pursue issues dealing with the crosscurrents in philosophy, poetry, literature, and the natural sciences.

In articulating his multi-disciplinary approach to issues across the spectrum of human learning Blaga was able to draw from many philosophical and cultural wells, including those that sprung up within the Western tradition and those that surfaced on Eastern soil during more ancient times. Blaga's knowledge of world philosophy and culture was broad as it was deep, and in drawing both from Western and Eastern wellsprings his thought is today appropriately nuanced to surmount the residual Eurocentrism that continues to inform certain cultural products of the West. Blaga's world-encompassing contributions move from East to West and from West to East, enriching the philosophical insights of both.

The implications of such a geo-philosophical breadth of discovery and reflection provides a sheet anchor against any sterile territorialisation that restricts the potential of philosophical conversations reaching beyond the barriers of city-states of the ancient world and the nation states of modernity. Its inner dynamic bodes well for the initiation of a cosmopolitanism that augers in the direction of genuine philosophical conversations across the self-isolating voices of ethnic and national enclaves. Differences regarding thought, discourse, and action will undoubtedly remain, but what will become prominent is the struggle and dynamics to communicate with others in spite of and often because of cultural differences, awakening us to the need to strive for a dialectically enriching conversation of world citizenry. Lucian Blaga can help us achieve such an awakening. The world owes an inestimable debt to the various editors, translators, and commentators for their dedication and diligence in having made possible the production and publication of *Lucian Blaga: Selected Philosophical Extracts*.

Calvin O. Schrag
Professor Emeritus, Purdue University, West Lafayette, Indiana

Chapter 1

Introduction:
Life and Philosophy

Even fifty years after his death Lucian Blaga is hardly known in the English-speaking world, save for his poetry. The aim of this volume is to present, for the first time in book form, sufficient translated extracts from his extensive philosophical publications to show the extent, depth, originality and continuing importance of his philosophical thinking

This Introduction consists of five sections: 1. Life and Publications; 2. An Outline of Blaga's Philosophy in its Contexts; 3. Its Impact at Home and Abroad; 4. Blaga in Relation to Contemporary Continental European Philosophy; 5. Blaga and Contemporary Anglophone Philosophy; 6. An Outline of the Selected Extracts. Inevitably there are some overlaps among them.

1. Life and publications

Lucian Blaga is one of the most prominent persons in the history of Romanian culture. A great poet and philosopher, his works had a decisive influence on the Romanian poetry of the 20th century and on the self-definition of the Romanian national consciousness, and represented a major contribution to the foundation of the metaphysics of knowledge, of the philosophy of unconscious categories and of the philosophy of cultural styles.

Lucian Blaga was born in Transylvania, on May 9th 1895. He was the ninth child of the parish priest (Romanian Orthodox Church) of Lancrăm, a village situated near Alba Iulia in Transylvania, at that time part of the Kingdom of Hungary within the Austro-Hungarian Empire. He attended high school and the School of Theology in Transylvania. Then he went to Vienna, where he attended the courses of the Faculty of Philosophy, getting his Ph.D. with a thesis on *Kultur und Erkenntnis* (*Culture and Knowledge*). At the age of 15, he published his first poems in the literary review *Tribuna* and at the age of 19, he published his first philosophical essay *Notes on*

Intuition in Bergson in *Review Românul* in Arad. In 1919 he published his first volume of poetry, *Poems of Light* and a volume of aphorisms, *Stones for my Temple*. In 1924 his first book of philosophy *The Philosophy of Style* was published. It was the beginning of a prolific career, which produced many volumes of poetry and philosophical works. The latter would finally constitute the four trilogies (*Trilogy of Cognition, Trilogy of Culture, Trilogy of Values, Cosmological Trilogy*), which define his philosophical system, articulated on central categories such as mystery, style and culture. His work also includes plays, a novel, essays, memoirs and aphorisms. Between 1924 and 1939 he was a press attaché, cultural counsellor and minister plenipotentiary in six European capitals. From 1939 to 1947 he was highly appreciated as the Professor of Philosophy of Culture at the University of Cluj, a position created especially for him. Elected a member of the Romanian Academy, Blaga delivered in the presence of King Carol II of Romania one of the most consistent and expressive reception speeches, *Eulogy to the Romanian Village*, a fundamental text for anyone who wants to understand the special character of the Romanian people. The response was given by another philosopher, Ion Petrovici. Blaga was also a brilliant translator of Goethe (*Faust*) and Lessing. The post-war Communist regime removed him from his chair at Cluj and appointed him as the librarian and a researcher at the University of Sibiu, now named after him, and where he had gone with others during the years when Hitler gave northern Transylvania back to Hungary. He was banned from publishing any philosophical work. Nominated for the Nobel Prize 1956 on the proposal of Bazil Munteanu (France) and Rosa del Conte (Italy), he was on the point of getting the award when the Communist government in Bucharest sent emissaries to Sweden to protest against his nomination with false political allegations.

He died in 1961 at Cluj, and was buried back in the churchyard at Lancrăm, where a fine statue of him in his academic gown stands by his grave. After his death his daughter, Dorli Blaga, began to republish his *Trilogies*, to which she added later works, all of which are now reprinted by Humanitas in Bucharest.

2. An outline of Blaga's philosophy in its contexts

A comparative analysis of Blaga's ideas within the context of modern orientations in thinking would define his position as kindred to and yet different from those of Kant, Goethe, Nietzsche, Spengler, Husserl, Berdiaev, Cassirer, Freud, Jung and Heidegger. His modern openings toward philosophy with polar concepts, and towards complementarity, define his conceptions as a special form of rationalism, ecstatic rationalism. Together with other Romanians—Vasile Conta, Mircea Florian, Stephane Lupasco, D. D. Roşca, Constantin Noica—Blaga outlines a certain type of discourse specific to Romanian philosophy between the wars, which gave new meanings to metaphysics, unconscious antimonies and relativity. In Blaga's opinion the supreme spiritual value is metaphysics.

> In metaphysical creation we can see the very crowning of philosophical thinking. We shall spare no effort in pleading in favour of such an appreciation. The metaphysician is the author of a world. Any philosopher who does not aim at becoming the author of a world simply betrays his own vocation; he may sometimes be a really brilliant thinker, still he would remain an advocate of non-fulfilment ... It is true that a metaphysical vision is never final; that is, no success makes useless a new attempt. A metaphysical vision represents an historical moment, meaning that in a way its fragility is inherent in its very conditions and structure ... We have to get accustomed to approaching metaphysical conceptions from a point of view different from that of regret for their perishability. We are then able to grasp that particular sensitivity of weighing a metaphysical vision according to its depth and inner harmony.

> We repeat: whenever we have to judge some metaphysical conception we are asked to use an immanent critique. Under such flashes of light, the transitoriness with which each metaphysical conception is stigmatised grows into a fatality which is inherent in even the most evident achievements of the human mind. Contrary to classic systems, this system I am working on has a symphonic character; it is not the system of a single idea, nor of a single formula; it is structured just like a many-steepled church. This system contains numerous intertwined main leitmotifs, that reiterate from one study to another and a rhythmically alternating succession. Eventually, all studies overflow as a metaphysical vision of the whole of existence; the last volume of each of the trilogies attempts to be a crowning of the others and a metaphysical turning to account of the problems discussed.[1]

For Blaga, metaphysics is something different from science and from philosophy with scientific aspects. 'Metaphysics is always a jump into the uncontrollable, a creation of imagination... experience plays here only the role of a veto when metaphysics contradicts it, but experience is not asked to check and positively control metaphysical conceptions'.[2]

In *Transcendental Censure*, Blaga admits that 'an absolute metaphysical principle' exists as well as an individuated cognition, their relationship being perceived as a relationship between productive existence and a produced existence, that is between the creator and the created, between an X that determines and a determined result. According to Blaga, the absolute metaphysical principle is what metaphysics has always taken to be substance, the absolute ego, the immanent reason, the unconscious, the consciousness etc., that is all that he calls 'the Great Anonymous' (or 'Anonym'). He is not interested in finding out whether the Great Anonymous is immanent or transcendent as related to existence, but in learning that the Great Anonymous is characterised by the central place taken in the system of existence. The thesis about the relationship between the Great Anonymous and personal cognition is thus formulated by the Romanian thinker: 'For reasons that pertain to existential balance, the great Anonymous defends himself and all the mysteries deriving hence, from aspirations of any individual cognition, creating between these and the existential mysteries a network of insulating factors. The insulating network placed between the existential mysteries and individuated cognition appears as censure'.[3]

The potentiality of dual thinking has been realised and represents a topical subject of debate at present, but an exegesis such as the one Blaga devoted to it in *The Dogmatic Aeon* and in his entire work, has not been repeated so far, at least not to our knowledge. Establishing his roots in ancient modalities of reflection, whether philosophical, religious or mystical and following its manifestations in the history of culture, the Romanian philosopher proved that dual, antinomic thinking is specific to man and becomes manifest in times of aeonic renewal, characterised by major shifts in spiritual paradigms. As a main feature of such periods of transition, Hellenism and the 20th century share it, as well as the aspiration to synthesis, the dovetailing of oriental and western thinking, the triumph of 'configuration' in science, the search for deep meanings of existence in myths and symbols, in new philosophical constructions and significations (the relativity of orientations in philosophy, the interest in the philosophy of history, the inauguration of a new ontology). Convinced that this way of intellectual ecstasis was the only one able to create the matrix of a new metaphysics, adapted to the spirit of a new aeon, Blaga tried out the power of the antinomic method in the very elaboration of his work. Thus, Blaga's system is built up around dual and complementary concepts such as consciousness and unconsciousness, enstatic and ecstatic intellect, Kantian and abyssal categories as duplicates, Luciferian and paradisiac types of knowledge, and anabasic and catabasic views of human destiny. The so-called dogmatic method, the method of 'transfigured antinomy', the complementary duality in fact, realises the shift in orientation from plus-knowledge to minus-knowledge, by applying the antinomic perspective to the dichotomy known-unknown. On this ground, it can be explained why the unknown as a whole is not decreased by the deduction of the known; on the contrary, it actually increases by being put into words, opening itself to new logical potentials. Antinomy, Blaga states, will bring forth the future cultural coherence, where science will open new mysteries 'by Luciferian knowledge', entering a new stylistic field, characterised by new orientations, horizons and values (of a systemic, contextualist, complementary type, we should add).

Within the contemporary intellectual contexts, when renowned scientists and philosophers (R. Thorn, E. Laszlo, I. Prigogine, M. Bunge, S. Lupasco, etc.) manifest interest in a new philosophy of nature, in an ontology of the human (psyche, social, moral), Blaga's metaphysics, as an ontological theory of culture, opens a surprisingly prolific philosophical horizon. The Archimedean point of his thinking lies in his conception of the categorical structure of the unconsciousness and of the stylistic matrix, the way stylistic categories function in the process of creation being the link among the philosophies of knowledge, culture and values, while his metaphysical construction represents the final fulfilment, in the horizon of mystery, of all his indisputably original philosophical approaches.

However, in company with important contemporary names in philosophy of science (Koyré, Collingwood, Kuhn, Prigogine, M. Polanyi, Rorty, Chomsky, Thorn etc.), Blaga's contributions are both essential and actual, as he investigated the cognitive dimensions of science in an ontological, cultural, historical and axiological context and realised the interdisciplinary integration of philosophy of science, on the one hand, and theory of knowledge, the philosophy of culture and axiology, on the other. As with recent theories of the 'innate' in knowledge, of 'historical entities' in the field of the dynamics of science, of the disciplinary matrices and contexts of the anthropology of epistemological outlooks, Blaga introduced many original and interesting ideas. Among them are: the stylistic and cultural approach to science, the theory of categorical doubles, the over-method and minus-knowledge, and differences and connections between science and philosophy. These ideas became even more relevant within the context of the dispute with the adepts of neo-positivism and the adepts of phenomenology. R. T. Allen, for example, notes from a comparative analysis between Polanyi and Blaga that:

> They were both interested in the deep structures of the mind and its knowledge, structures of which, they both emphasised, we are not normally aware yet which guide our proximate knowledge and action. Both of them were thus radically opposed to those Empiricist theories which, in Locke's words, regard the mind as a 'blank tablet' passively receiving 'impressions', and to Positivist philosophies which deny the very existence of frameworks of thought and interpretation of experience. Equally, and unlike Kant, they had a sense of the historical and developing character of those structures and frameworks, yet, unlike many post-modern thinkers, they also emphasised our commitment to truth and to revealing the real world that is independent of our knowing. These are the lines that any genuine philosophy must take.[3]
>
> In particular, they both recognised that reality transcends our cognitive abilities and that is cannot be confined within any formulae. Blaga regards mystery as an essential and distinctive feature of man and human awareness, a permanent background to all our knowledge. He criticises theories of cognition, and especially of science, which reduce all knowledge to what he calls Type 1 (or 'paradisiac') knowledge, in which certain categories, not varying greatly across history, are applied fairly straight-forwardly in perception and action. In contrast, science also requires Type 2 (or 'Luciferian') knowledge which applies deeper categories, relating to man's distinctive existence within a horizon of mystery and revealing those mysteries. These categories are much less fixed and general, and themselves guided by yet deeper, 'abyssal', categories which form a 'stylistic field'. Blaga rejects the Positivist characterisation of

such categories, e.g. teleology in biology, as 'useful fictions', and stresses that they function to reveal mysteries. Polanyi likewise emphasises the roles of intellectual frameworks and the activity of the knower in the formation of our knowledge, and also is aware of their variability while insisting that we aim at truth 'with universal intent', although we can never quite get there, a point that Blaga also makes. Polanyi again criticised the 'pseudo-substitutions' offered for the notion of truth ('economy', 'simplicity', Kant's 'regulative ideas') which tacitly trade on the notion of truth which they supposed to replace. He also maintained that reality outruns our attempts to know it and that it cannot be confined within our formulae.[4]

In order to seize the entire novelty of Blaga's vision, the analysis of his sources (the morphology of culture, the philosophy of life, psycho-analysis) is relevant, as well as the comparative approach in connection with structuralism (Lévy-Bruhl, Foucault), existentialism (Heidegger, Jaspers) or with postmodernism (Rorty).

As C. O. Schrag states,

Lucian Blaga was able to marshal conceptual and spiritual resources for addressing the philosophical situation of our time. It were as though Blaga anticipated the intersection/confrontation of the modernist and postmodernist cultures at our own *fin-de-siecle*. And it is his notion of 'transfigured antinomy' that we find to be of particular pertinence for addressing the issues at hand.[5]

In a conference at Arizona University E. Ramsey describes the manner in which Blaga relates to the philosophical perspective of Emerson, the American philosopher. In this respect he emphasises that Blaga construes a special concept of man:

The fact that man has become Man, that is creative subject, thanks to a decisive ontological mutation, could, of course, signify that man completed evolution which works through biological mutation; it could therefore mean that no superior biological species is possible beyond him.[6]

The dynamic of a transfigured antinomy is such that the differences at issue retain their integrity while being transfigured in such a manner as to be comprehended through a complementarity of perspectives, articulated via a new logic of opposition. Now it was the genius of Blaga to discern the applicability of the dynamics of transfigured antinomies not only across the specialised areas of the physical sciences, but also with the developing fields of micro- and macro-biology, as well as within the wider cultural existence of the human species. That which strikes us as being of particular moment in Blaga's understanding and use of the notion of transfigured antinomy is its relevance for addressing the problematic of modernity versus postmodernity of our time. On the one hand we are presented with a logic of identity, with its claims for a unity of knowledge, a totality of explanation, and a universal commensurability; and on the other hand we encounter the partisans of difference, plurality, heterogeneity, incommensurability, and historical particularity. The modernist would have us keep the vision of a universal logos wherewith to secure the stable contents of knowledge; the postmodernist, positioned against the logocentrism of modernity, would have us scatter the universal logos to the wind and make do with the heterogeneity of language games and the relativity of historically specific beliefs and practices. With our notion of transversal rationality cum communication we are in a position to mediate between the universal logos of modernity and the anti-logos of postmodernity, utilizing the resources of an expanded reason that is able to extend across the differences of beliefs and perspectives, converging with them without achieving coincidence at a point of identity. And it is a with a measure of philosophical excitement that we have found a family resemblance of our notion of transversal rationality in Lucian Blaga's notion of transfigured antinomy.

To re-think the human world from the perspective of the man-nature-culture triad, as Blaga does in his *Trilogy of Knowledge*, means to create new philosophical discipline of noology concerned with the uniqueness of the human, with the ontological meaning of culture and of metaphor, with the structure of the noosphere (the layer of ideas that surrounds the earth). No less important is Blaga's critical analysis of biologist theories (Arnold Gehlen, Paul Alsberg[7]), which shows his difference from Bergson, Freud, Nietzsche, and Cassirer.

Equally noteworthy are his visions of the philosophy of art (the law of nontransponsibility, polar and vector values) and of religion as a form of culture. Conceived as an ontological mutation, culture is the standpoint of the building and architecture of Blaga's system.

Man exists as a creative subject in the universe through culture alone: he became a constituent part of his being. Therefore philosophy, as both knowledge and metaphysical construction, science, as cognitive act and cultural creation, noology as investigation of the uniqueness of the human and the genesis of metaphor, all lead, through the stylistic matrix, to man as being in the centre of cultural values, which, in their turn, are constituent parts of each spiritual aeon.

The influence of Neo-Kantianism, of Hegel, of Goethe, of the philosophy of life and of the morphology of culture on Blaga, as well as the originality of his thinking, can be traced in philosophy but also in his literary work. Neither his poetry, a lyrical expression of the ontological mutation within an inner tension due to the relationship between man and Cosmos, nor his plays, which project human drama on the level of the universal Whole and reveal the passage from appearance to essence, from the momentary to the transcendent, can be grasped without taking into account his spiritual biography, and his philosophical vision.

3. Its impact at home and abroad

Around thirty monographs and numerous studies on Lucian Blaga's works have been published in Romania. The place of Lucian Blaga's works within the context of philosophical thinking between the wars in Romania is a singular one, which partly explains their more or less sinuous 'destiny' after the author's death. His posterity recorded the most various and antagonistic attitudes toward his work, even extreme ones occasionally, from apology to a negation. The diversity of the comments represents in itself a proof of the complexity and the far-reaching implications of his work. Obviously, the critical and thorough analysis of his works is far from being completed. New facets of the text unveil themselves for the observant reader all the time. Honest and unprejudiced exegeses, dedicated to the thorough examination of the intrinsic philosophical value of his works, reveals the specificity of his system and method, as well as the central concepts of his thinking: mystery, style, transfigured antinomy, the Great Anonym, the categories of unconsciousness.

As did Brâncuși, Țuculescu, Ion Barbu and other Romanian artists close to the vision of the Mioritic space,[8] Blaga retraces the origins of creation in search for the stylistic matrices, for the primordial patterns, for the layer of genesis, a universal vision of the organic in an endless dissemination of variants around some imagistic centres, some cardinal ideas. Through his entire work, Blaga valued the creative genius of the Romanian people and sustained the self-consciousness and dignity of Romanian culture its specificity among other European cultures and emphasised its values in their entire complexity and continuity. As early as 1936, he was writing:

> The close and tenacious examination of our folk culture led us to the gratifying certitude of the existence of a Romanian stylistic matrix. Its latencies barely perceived justify the conclusion that we have a high cultural potential. All we can say, without fear of being contradicted by further evolutions, is that we are the bearers of huge possibilities. All we can state, without violating lucidity, is that we trust we have been assigned to enlighten, with our flower to come, a corner of the Earth. All we can hope, without making ourselves prey to illusions, is the pride of some historic spiritual initiatives that would flow, from time to time, like sparks over the heads of other peoples.[9]

Blaga's philosophy has been frequently reprinted, and discussed abroad as well in Romania. After the Italian version of his book, *Horizon and Style* (*Orizzonte e stile*) was published in 1946, *L'Age de l'homme* Publishing House published *L'Eon dogmatique* (1988); then *Librairie du savoir* (Paris) published *L'Élogue du village roumain* (1989), *L'etre historique* (1990) and *Les differentiels divines* (1990). Other studies included in the *Trilogies* were translated and published in French by a team from the Sorbonne. The critical bibliography of Blaga's works also includes titles published outside Romania such as: *Profili di estetica europea: Lucian Blaga, Gaston Bachelard, Carl Gustav Jung,* Casa editrice Oreste Bayes, Rome, 1971; *Contributions a l'histoire de la versification roumaine: La prosodie de Lucian Blaga,* Akademiai Kyodo, Budapest, 1972. Beginning in 1932, twenty-three foreign encyclopaedias and lexicons have mentioned his work. *The Encyclopaedia of Philosophy* (ed. Edwards, 1962) underlines the originality and harmonious architecture of his philosophical system in the article on Romanian (Rumanian) philosophy.

> The most gifted and original thinker has been Lucian Blaga, the only Rumanian philosopher to have completed and extremely complex system, including a highly personal metaphysics, a new theory of knowledge, and a detailed

morphology of culture. In this ambitious construction Blaga utilised myths, symbols, and ideas from popular Rumanian traditions, both religious and secular. For the first time, the autochtonous heritage of Rumania found philosophical expression.[10]

Antonio Banfi dedicates to Blaga a whole chapter in his book *Filosofia dell'Arte*, and names him 'one of the most vivid and original contemporary philosophers'. A society for the philosophy of style was created at the Sorbonne, bearing Blaga's name.

And now a full-length study has been published in English, Michael Jones' *The Metaphysics of Religion: Lucian Blaga and Contemporary Philosophy*,[11] which includes a general introduction to his philosophy as well as its particular topic.

As time goes by, Blaga's work proves to be an endless source of meanings and significations in the confrontation with new trends in thinking and new artistic models. It brings to unsettled controversies the multitude of approaches and interpretations which it generates by its vivid strength, the sign of the great spiritual creations, which defy centuries and paradigms by the very fact that they remain open to rational and sensible understanding, and that, in spite of accumulations of data in knowledge, they preserve their cognitive challenge, their ability to incite the mind to search for new solutions of the central mystery of our Being.

4. Blaga and contemporary Continental European philosophy: history, knowledge and culture: the privileges of human being

In order to understand the situation of Lucian Blaga's philosophy in relation to continental philosophy we should briefly portray the characteristics of the latter.

When we turn to *The Oxford Handbook of Continental Philosophy*,[12] we see that 'Continental philosophy' is first of all 'philosophy in Continental Europe in the nineteenth and twentieth century, best understood as connected waves of traditions, some of which overlap, but no one of which dominate all the others'. This specific 'assembly' of existentialism, phenomenology, German idealism, structuralism, post-structuralism, French feminism and the Frankfurt School, which make up Continental philosophy, can be also defined through several themes: the rejection of scientism; the tendency towards historicism; the power of conscious human agency to change the contingencies and ultimately the world; and the emphasis on metaphilosophy.

Each of these descriptive dimensions applies to Lucian Blaga's works. First, his philosophy is not scientism. Situating at the core of his philosophical system the idea of mystery which influences both his philosophical perspective of human being and his perspective on knowledge, Blaga succeeds in emphasising the distinctiveness of the philosophical method in comparison to that of the natural sciences, for instance, in *The Divine Differentials*, in 'The Uniqueness of Man' or in *The Genesis of Metaphor and the Meaning of Culture* and in other writings. At the same time, Blaga rejecting scientism does not reject science itself. It is rather a difference of degree between science and metaphysics. We recall that Blaga's example, for his concept of antinomy was that of the new physics of light where light was conceived in two ways, both 'corpuscular' and 'wave-like', an example of the acknowledgement of mystery and its centrality to the newer (philosophical) modes of scientific understanding. His metaphysical theory of knowledge is teleological and axiological, not confined to identifying the limits of knowledge. Knowledge is related to consciousness, its values and finalism. But this finalism does not cancel the creative destiny of the human being and for this reason we can say that finalism borders consciousness, but (paradoxically) it does not characterise it.

As well, Blaga embraces historicism. For him,

> History is in the metaphysical order and that of the finalities of existence, this manner of living and creating of man as a being dangerous to the Great Anonymous and as being rejected by the Great Anonymous via the pre-emptive dispositions undertaken once and forever. [...] History is in its every moment this sort of existence of the great intentions, an existence imploded, because its only means of accomplishment at hand are turning unceasingly against it. History does not have a purpose, a terminus, for which it longs and which is a future end. History is waved, as an ontological mutation in the Universe, and it will not end, but with the end of man, being and remaining history, entirely, in each and every moment.[13]

Blaga relates historicism to a specific human mythical consciousness. This specificity is a mark of the pre-historical mysterious times. Consequently, this pre-historical hallmark influences human

Introduction: Life and Philosophy

history and it is a privilege of the creative (and dangerous) human being. 'Myth is a creation of man in relation to his coordinates, specifically and wholly human, emerging in the order of the human existence.'[14] We should emphasise here the concept of order: its main meaning of structure and sequential arrangement is complemented with another meaning more metaphorical, of nature and even essence of being. Blaga's historicism is often compared to Spengler's, and Blaga refers to Spengler, and Berdyaev[15] in his works, but for Blaga history is not necessarily oriented toward progress and civilisation, nor is it valued as a superior stage of culture.

More recently, Henrieta Șerban and Eric Gilder have argued for connections between Blaga's historicism and Richard Rorty's ironism.[16] The Rortian notion of ironism was either misunderstood or ignored, treated hastily as irony (and irony is an obstacle in the way of solidarity), even by very good analysts of philosophy, such as Simon Critchley. Rorty's definition presents an 'ironist' as:

> Someone who fulfils three conditions: (1) She has radical and continuing doubts about the final vocabulary she currently uses, because she has been impressed by other vocabularies, vocabularies taken as final by people or books she has encountered; (2) she realizes that argument phrased in her present vocabulary can neither underwrite nor dissolve these doubts; (3) insofar as she philosophizes about her situation, she does not think that her vocabulary is closer to reality than others, that is in touch with a power not herself. Ironists who are inclined to philosophize see choice between vocabularies made neither within a neutral and universal meta-vocabulary nor by an attempt to fight one's way past appearances to the real, but simply by playing the new off against the old.[17]

So, the ironist should take a philosophical stand against the world, and enjoy creatively other vocabularies as a continuous inspiration to their own vocabulary, continuously 'under construction'. This is the essence of philosophical thinking and living according to Blaga, too, precisely because the mystery and the transcendental censorship prevent the arrival at the essence of things, if that exists:

> Philosophical thinking, through its buildings and its debris, through its delusions and disappointments that it does

provoke to us all, through the suspicions and presentiments that it communicates to us, through the ever deeper inquiries that it occasions and invites, will mean therefore for the human genre an unlimited surplus of lucidity, its different stages being equivalent to as many 'awakenings' from the infinite sleep where our being floats.[18]

In other words, philosophy is re-examination of things and the refusal to embrace ultimate positions, the effort of continuous awakening (in Rorty, the awakening corresponds to the continuous adjustment of vocabulary), time and time again. Simon Critchley makes a similar point himself when he writes: 'The freedom of the philosopher consists in either moving freely from topic to topic or simply spending years returning to the same topic out of perplexity, fascination and curiosity.'[19] History and being in the world are intimately interconnected things. For Blaga man both creates history and is its object, while history is an ontological consequence of man's life in the horizon of mystery, for revelation. History is man's destiny.

Rorty's post-liberalism starts with this freedom of thought manifest in vocabulary as a refusal of being to be limited in spite of the real, political or traditional limitations. Blaga's human being manifests its freedom historically, in spite of the limitations, too. For Lucian Blaga, the power of conscious human agency to change the contingencies of existence is provided by the capacity of the human being to both live creatively and create in spite of the limitations of consciousness, and by the transcendental censorship (because while acting and creating, the Great Anonymous starts seeing the human actor as a competitor). The human being is a creative being according to Blaga and all the creations, cultural, metaphysical, scientific or even material, retain the traces and influences of the abyssal categories, related to conscious categories, but structured in a different manner. The unconscious is correspondingly related to the conscious. Similarly, the physical and cosmic categories are reminiscent of the abyssal ones. For instance, the *doina* song describes a specific undula space, the same valley/hill alternate design which expresses a specific, Romanian, undulating lyricism. Born in the magical thinking and creation of God, man is not estranged from magic and creation, although man experiences limitations inclusively from the transcendent censorship, presented to a greater detail in the volume. Thus, we can notice the similarity of the tasks and their scope for the Blagian historical being and the

Rortian ironist: they have to understand the world anew and their purpose is infinitely demanding.

Blaga notices that modernity brings about a generous and flexible understanding for times and places, though more noticeable in what concerns the concept of style, as approached by Simmel, Riegl, Worringer, Frobenius, Spengler, Keyserling, Wölfflin[20] and others, who used style almost as a cognitive category, useful for evaluating the world and the products of the human mind:

> We live in a period of generous understanding for all times and places and of a flexible sensitivity to style. This is an aspect which we should take into account if we wish to relieve the complex of inferiority which holds us in its grip. In no other period could Europeans pride themselves on such a capacity of sympathy and understanding for spiritual products from other times and other places. In no other period did sensitivity manifest such universal responsiveness. This power of conscious understanding has even attained the impressive proportions of a record and we do not know how it could ever be surpassed.[21]

And last but not least, Lucian Blaga places an emphasis on metaphilosophy. In this volume the reader is introduced to his metaphysical vision of existence leading the philosopher to create a system of philosophy structured in trilogies around the concept of mystery interrogated within the space of philosophy of science. From this foundation knowledge is conceived dually: knowledge built within the frame of the given universe in order to complete the blanks of the unknown ('paradisiac') and knowledge within the frame of mystery where the given world is composed of traces or signals of mysteries ('Luciferian'). Metaphysics is seen as different from the philosophy of science; because in metaphysics the role of experience is minimal while in the philosophy of science it plays a more important role in both types of knowledge. The extract from *The Dogmatic Aeon* in this volume explores the meanings of apparently diverse worlds, Asiatic and Christian, combining religious visions, with scientific and philosophical ideas, abstract and mythological, identifying correspondences between these worlds and founding a new ontology and a reformed theory of knowledge, implying relativism and an important role for the philosophy of history. Metaphysics is changing according to the historical characteristics of the times. For Blaga the philosopher is situated between abstraction and myth, and this specific situation influences the particularities of philosophy: 'Without difficulty a kinship could also be established between the symbolist-allegorical method so current in Gnostic thinking and the method of the same sort at home in modern psychoanalysis: "the far-off analogy," cultivated with eager interest both then and now.'[22] Philosophy is the product of the ecstatic intellect, which is capable of 'plus', 'zero' and 'minus' knowledge, the one which creates a tension between the apparent and cryptic dimensions of things in order to investigate them and find their proper place within the order of things. Philosophy, as mathematics, is a construction of knowledge, which, unlike mathematics, is affected by the spiritual long durations, reverberating in cultural styles.

5. Blaga and contemporary Anglophone philosophy

The question inevitably arises as to what claims Blaga and his philosophy may have in the context of contemporary Anglophone philosophy, and especially Analytic philosophy.

1. Blaga offers what Anglophone philosophy often lacks, viz., a more synthetic and synoptic approach. We tend to break up the subject-matter of philosophy into relatively distinct disciplines, especially as regards the study of man himself. We have philosophy of mind, which also deals with questions of the relation of mind to body, though at present often confined to speculations about brains, and occasionally broadens out to a philosophy of action; we have ethics which treats of human duty, and less often of the human good; but we do not cultivate a philosophical anthropology which brings together these facets of human being and which also locates and differentiates man in relation to the rest of existence. Of course there are exceptions, such as Charles Taylor, Alastair MacIntyre and Robert Nozick, but for the most part we deal piecemeal and serially with separate questions and problems without trying to bring them together.

Blaga, while also dealing with more specific matters in the several volumes of his Trilogies and in the studies which comprise each, also brings them together, and that in two ways. Explicitly, as in the metaphysical essays of *The Divine Differentials* and the anthropological ones of *Anthropological Aspects* and 'The Uniqueness of Man' in *The Genesis of Metaphor and the Meaning of Culture*; and implicitly, as he himself pointed out in his 'Philosophical Self-Interpretation', by the interweaving of themes that recur from volume to volume, as will be seen from the titles of the essays in each volume as given in the Bibliography.

Yet Blaga avoids also the two dangers of the more synthetic approach: immediate generalisation which produces impressively sounding *dicta* yet fails to test them, and moving in a world of abstractions without any concrete illustrations. Because this publication is an anthology, Blaga will inevitably appear more 'dogmatic' and abstract than he really is, for inevitably the focus is upon those summary passages in which his principal ideas and theses are formulated, to the neglect of the extended elaborations, arguments and illustrations. We have therefore included nearly all of 'The Mioritic Space' as an example of how Blaga seeks empirical illustration and support for his one of his contentions.

Furthermore, Blaga situates himself in history. *The Dogmatic Aeon* is a survey of the major forms and developments in European thought since the Hellenistic period, which culminates in a consideration of the general problems raised by the theory of relativity, the philosophical significance of which Blaga immediately grasped. It then gives outlines of new ways of thinking, such as 'transfigured antinomy' as prefigured in Christian theology but now generalised, and 'minus cognition' which deepens mysteries, and also of a wholly new intellectual climate, a 'post-dogmatic' age we might say, which Blaga sees as emerging. Likewise in *Science and Creation*, Blaga surveys different conceptions of science that have appeared in history, as well as aesthetic styles.

2. As a more specific example of Blaga's equally analytic and synthetic approach, we may cite his treatment of the theme of culture. Man essentially exists in a cultural world which he creates, inherits and transmits. But we do not consider culture in its own right, whereas 'the philosophy of culture' was the title of the chair created for him at Cluj when he turned from diplomacy to teaching. Consequently, Blaga considers notable cultural forms such as religion, myth, magic, art, and science, but not just serially. In them he finds the expression of 'style'. For us 'style' at best would be a theme for aesthetics and even then would probably be shuffled off to the history of art. Yet for Blaga it has a profound significance. For, abandoning those epistemologies which assume a passive mind, and being fully aware of what we bring to bear upon experience, Blaga sees 'style' as a central feature of all human activity. Long before Kuhn introduced us to 'paradigms' in science, Blaga showed how style pervades all the activities of man, science as much as art.

It is that which constitutes culture, man's specific mode of being, and which differentiates one culture or period from another.

3. Anglophone philosophy, like most philosophy since Descartes, has been primarily concerned with knowledge, and especially with 'justifying' claims to knowledge, and in turn by seeking its 'foundations'. Now that we are supposed to have abandoned the last at least, there may be more sympathy for Blaga's approach which, by and large, is to focus on the emergence and differentiation of new forms of knowledge, and upon the *knowing*, cognition, rather than upon the *known*, *how* we know rather than how we *know*. Blaga is especially concerned to differentiate two forms of cognition, 'paradisiac' and 'Luciferian', the latter being peculiar to man, and to emphasise the category of 'mystery', which is not a problem to be solved but something to be revealed as the mystery that it is, and perhaps to be deepened, by 'minus-cognition'. Blaga's initial example, which led him to this formulation, is the antinomy of the new physics of light which required it to be thought of as both 'corpuscular' and 'wave-like', terms which exclude each other. What is required at that point is not yet more 'plus knowledge', of adding facts to facts to be understood by existing conceptions and explanations, but the recognition of this mystery which has been revealed, a mystery which lies beyond the scope of our present modes of understanding. Minus knowledge is a function of Luciferian knowledge which is not content with resting happily in what is already known ('enstatic' intellect) but seeks to go beyond it ('ecstatic' intellect). What minus cognition recognises is that, firstly, we have encountered something that we cannot understand with existing methods, principles and conceptions, and which calls for a leap into the unknown and to a higher level of thought, and, secondly, that, even when we have attained such a higher level, there still remains the core of the mystery itself which outruns our knowledge of it and our attempts, inevitably partial, to clarify it by our theoretical constructions. Blaga's theory has been termed an 'ecstatic rationalism', which is to say that it has none of the absolutist pretensions usually associated with rationalism, which would exhibit a Luciferian conceit in our own abilities.

Blaga is therefore one of a number of philosophers in the 20th century, such as Merleau-Ponty, Polanyi and Heidegger, who have realised that human knowledge, precisely because it deals with a real world independent of itself, has its inevitable limits, horizons and tacit dimensions, and that its operations cannot be reduced to sets of explicit rules. Algorithms apply only to what is routine. The novel, especially that which breaks our existing rules, requires a creative invention of new procedures and conceptions altogether, which no existing rule can tell us how to do. Nor does our success at doing this once or twice permit us to imagine that at any point we have reached a final and absolute level of understanding on which no further mysteries will be encountered and where, from now onwards, all will be routine, the dream of modern epistemology from Descartes onwards. Blaga's account of the negative side of Luciferian knowledge (its temptation to think that now it has dissolved mystery forever), can be applied equally to Hegelian claims to absolute knowledge devoid of mystery, and to Positivist and Reductionist claims that what cannot meet their requirements for clear and precise knowledge is therefore either non-existent or not worth knowing (e.g. E. L. Thorndike's explicit claim that what cannot be measured is unreal).

As will be seen in the extract from 'The Divine Differentials', Blaga provides a metaphysical explanation for these permanent upper limits on human knowledge, the persistence of mystery: viz., that it is the result of a 'transcendental censorship' imposed by the 'Great Anonym' to prevent men becoming gods and thus rivalling him and causing cosmic anarchy. Whether or not we accept that, and Blaga, as also will be seen, held that there is a certain freedom in metaphysical construction which can only be falsified and not proved by experience, there is much that can be learned from his theory of cognition and which converges with other developments in philosophy in the 20th century.

We also note that Blaga, by applying something very close to Popper's principle of falsification to metaphysics, would reject Popper's use of it to demarcate science from non-science. Blaga was not constrained by Positivist rejections of all metaphysics, and such rejections are simply refusals on the Positivists' part to spell out and submit to examination what they in fact and unquestioningly take to be the ultimate constituents or sources of the world and the ultimate levels of explanation. Blaga at least tried to offer an explanation of why mystery is an inevitable ingredient in human knowledge.

4. In particular Blaga goes beyond Kant, with his fixed and invariable scheme of categories, to an additional set of categories in the unconscious, in partial or 'para-' correspondence with the former, a set which are far from invariant. These deeper or 'abyssal'

categories have the function of a 'stylistic matrix', that is, of generating the 'styles' which colour and control our ways of apprehending and acting within the world. For example, Merleau-Ponty, for one, has shown how we do not live in an abstract and undifferentiated geometrical space, though the formulation of such a space is a great human achievement, but in a space orientated and vectorised by the lived body. But Blaga, following morphologists of culture and going beyond them in linking their proposals to a general theory of knowledge, also discerns different ways in which space, and also time, have been unconsciously perceived in the lived experience of different peoples and ages as manifested in their works. Blaga thus combines an interest in essential structures of the mind with full awareness of the variability of more specific ways in which they have manifested themselves in history, a combination which is likely to be particularly helpful in the 'post-foundationalist' and 'post-modernist' climate of today.

In the very act of suggesting some ways in which Blaga's philosophy merits the attention of English-speaking philosophers, we have probably put a certain sort of 'hard-headed', 'no nonsense', philosopher completely off it. We can easily imagine such a one bristling at Blaga's terminology of 'paradisiac' and 'Luciferian' knowledge, 'integration into mystery', 'abyssal categories of the unconscious', 'stylistic matrix', 'Mioritic space', and so on, let alone Blaga's metaphysical interests and terms–'the Great Anonym', 'divine differentials' and 'transcendental censorship'. Such a philosopher would feel himself justified in dismissing Blaga at the outset as just another obscurantist, mystery-mongering, poetic, metaphorical, and typically Latin pseudo-philosopher. When he learns that Blaga was also a poet (one of Romania's finest) and a playwright, then his worst fears will be confirmed.

It is true that Blaga wrote philosophy in something of a poetic manner, just as he wrote poetry on philosophical themes, and, as usual with Latin writers, one cannot in translation make him sound like a native speaker of English, unless one substitutes quite another voice for his. But the playful spirit in Blaga cuts both ways: if he seems to like using a colourful terminology, and to delight in metaphysical construction for its own sake on his part and that of others, he also sits lightly to it. As he said in one of his aphorisms (quoted below), he was the freest of his followers. We should therefore look through and beyond the words to what he was talking about, and not reject all of his philosophy if we dislike the language used in some of it.

6. About this collection

The selections of the principal studies included in Blaga's trilogies have been arranged in a certain order, meant to facilitate the understanding of his philosophical system. The best introduction to Blaga is Blaga himself, which is why we begin with an extract from the manuscript of the conference on his philosophical self-presentation delivered by him when he was appointed Professor of Philosophy of Culture, in 1938. The text expresses what many other exegetes had tried to demonstrate, namely that his system does not explain only one single idea but his main leitmotifs intertwine and reiterate from one study to another, with a rhythmic alternation. The ideas presented in the first two volumes of each trilogy are crowned by a metaphysical perspective in each of the third volumes. The author's appreciation is clearly expressed here, namely that his main achievement, having roots throughout all his poetic or philosophical work, is represented by the metaphysics of knowledge.

The extract from *The Dogmatic Aeon*, defines the contemporary era as generating a new aeon, a new paradigm and pattern of knowledge and creation. Blaga reveals the resemblance between our age and the Hellenistic one, both producers of aeons as consisting in the fact that they both share the vocation for syntheses, the combination of Asian and European thinking, the search for an universal signification in various and dissonant ways, the co-existence of doctrines combining Asian and Christian religious visions with scientific and philosophical ideas, the combination of the abstract with the mythological, the search for morphological correspondences between different parts of the Universe under the form of 'typical configuration', the birth of a new ontologism and the reform of epistemology, originating relativity and the taste for the philosophy of history. The eschatological feeling, of the end of the world, and the aeonic one, of the beginning of a new spiritual world, is present throughout Blaga's philosophy, which mirrored the spirit of the time during which he created it.

The selections continue with an extract from *The Great Anonym*, where Blaga defines ontologically the Great Anonym, the central concept of his system, as 'metaphysical centre of existence', the guarantor of universal equilibrium, as a being in itself, with no attributes, whose will limits creation and forbids any man from knowing too much of the Great Anonym. Epistemologically, the Great Anonym is the one who intensifies mystery and generates negative thinking and an endless theogonic reproduction. Blaga traces the origins and limits of human knowledge, as determined by forces in transcendental censorship.

In *The Divine Differentials* an original syncretic vision is outlined. Cosmological, ontological and epistemological at the same time, it tries to describe the genetic techniques of the Great Anonym, who creates the world through the limitation and the disintegration of the divine being. The emission and thinking of the object generate chronological and spatial individuations. A divine differential represents, in Blaga's vision, the equivalent of an infinitesimal fragment of the autarchic, trans-spatial Wholeness of the Great Anonym. The divine differentials are generalisations of scientific differentials, but are limiting concepts. Blaga tried to replace the idea of the beginning as 'deed' or 'word' with that of the beginning as categorical detachment of the generating divinity from its own creative potential. Experience cannot corroborate metaphysics, but it can contradict it. The value of falsification is assigned a cosmological meaning by Blaga.

Blaga's epistemological ideas and the reform he initiates by his anti-reductionism, anti-positivism and anti-logicism are illustrated by the extract from 'Integration with Mystery' from Transcendental Censorship, 'Minus-Cognition' from *Luciferian Knowledge*, 'Two Types of Knowledge' and 'The Stylistic Field' from *Science and Creation*. The category of mystery, which Blaga locates right in the core of the theory of knowledge, also represents the principal connection with his metaphysical theory. Mystery is the core of the metaphysics of knowledge because it expresses the consciousness of an essential absence. As a category like substance, mind or time, mystery also represents an idea in the negative, a singular idea by means of which the power of transcending existing conceptions and frameworks is permitted to Luciferian knowledge. Integration with mystery takes place in three ways: the attenuation, making permanent and extension of the unknown. All philosophers so far, says Blaga, have felt the overall presence of mystery, yet they have been afraid of its existence, so that they have tried to annihilate it by negation. The novelty of Blaga's metaphysics resides in his accepting this permanent presence of mystery and, since every philosophy is born under the species of a category, his philosophy is built up under the species of mystery.

In the 'Genesis of Metaphor' and in 'The Uniqueness of Man' from *The Genesis of Metaphor and the Meaning of Culture* we pass to man and what distinguishes him from the rest of the world, especially from animals. They exist in the immediate and the demands of merely bodily existence. But man exists 'in mystery and for revelation', to bring forth, beyond any need for preserving his existence, what at present he does not know, and, beyond that, his awareness that there are things in the world which he cannot render wholly lucid. Man's consciousness is also informed by 'abyssal categories', a significant part of which is a 'stylistic matrix' which necessarily expresses itself in historical and cultural diversity.

The theme of style and its meaning continues in extracts from 'The Phenomenon of Style and Methodology', 'The Stylistic Matrix' and 'The Axiological Accent' from *Horizon and Style*, and an extract from *The Mioritic Space*, that display Blaga's anthropological and philosophical vision of culture.

The extracts conclude with a selection of those of his aphorisms which reflect something of his philosophical interests and themes.

In an appendix we present a glossary which will provide ready reference for detailed explanations of his special terms, followed by bibliographies of his philosophical books, each with a list of the contents, translations of all his works, and studies of his philosophy. Finally, we hope that this anthology will generate interest in Blaga and prepare the way for further translations, of complete volumes and not just extracts.

Angela Botez, Henrieta Anişoara Şerban, R. T. Allen

Notes

1. *On Philosophical Consciousness*, pp. 24-25.

2. *Philosophical Self-Presentation*, see below p.

3. 'The Metaphysical Form of Knowledge,' *The Trilogy of Knowledge*, vol. VIII, pp. 532-533. See also Lucian Blaga, *Trilogia cunoașterii*, (*Trilogy of Knowledge*). Bucharest: Ed. Minerva, 1983, pp. 74-75.

4. 'Some Notes on Michael Polanyi and Lucian Blaga', *Romanian Review*, 1/1996, p. 14.

5. Philosophy at the End of the 20th Century with a Note on Blaga,' *Romanian Review*, No. 1/1996.

6. Ramsey, E., 'The Interaction of Cultures. Blaga in Arizona,' *Annals* ARS, nos. 1-2 (2013)

7. Arnold Gehlen (1904-76): German philosopher, sociologist and anthropologist.

Paul Alsberg (1883-1965): German doctor and philosophical anthropologist. Emigrated to England in 1934.

8. 'Mioritic space': from 'Miorița', 'The Ewe Lamb', the best-known Romanian folk ballad. Blaga holds that it embodies the Romanian experience of space as undulating, which stems from life in the Transylvanian uplands crossed by long series of hills and valleys. See Chap. 10 below.

9. Botez, Angela, 'Lucian Blaga and His Philosophy,' *Annals* ARS, nos. 1-2 (2009).

10. New York: Macmillan and the Free Press, 1967.

11. Cranbury, NJ, Associated University Presses, 2010.

12. Eds Brian Leiter and Michael Rosen, Oxford: Oxford University Press, 2007.

13. 'The Metaphysics of History'. In: *The Cosmological Trilogy*, Works, vol. 11, 1980-8, pp. 487-489.

14. *Trilogia Culturii* (*Trilogy of Culture*). Bucharest: Ed. Minerva, 1985, p. 331

15. Nikolai Berdyaev (1874-1948): Exiled Russian, Christian Existentialist, religious and political philosopher.

Hermann Alexander, Graf Keyserling (1880-1946): a Baltic German philosopher who also wrote on style.

Oswald Spengler, 1880-1936, German author of *The Decline of the West* (1918-23) in which eight 'High Cultures', which all go through the same cycles of birth, development, fulfilment, decay and death, are said to be the real subject of history.

16. Botez, Angela, 'The Postmodern Anti-Rationalism (Polanyi, Blaga, Rorty)'. *Revue roumaine de philosophie*, nos.1-2 (1997) and Șerban, Henrieta A., and Eric Gilder. 'Blaga and Rorty. The Historical

Being and the Ironism.' *Revue roumanine de philosophie*, nos. 1-2 (2006): 19-29.

17. Rorty, Richard. 'Private Irony and Liberal Hope', in Walter Brogan, James Risser (eds.), *American Continental Philosophy. A Reader*. Bloomington and Indianapolis: Indiana University Press, 2000, p.46 (44-66).

18. 'Schita unei autoreprezentari', in A. Botez, *Dimensiunea metafizică a operei lui Lucian Blaga*. Bucharest: Scientific Publishing House, 1996, p. 29.

19. Critchley, Simon, *Infinitely Demanding: Ethics of Commitment, Politics of Resistance (Radical Thinkers)*. London, New York: Verso, 2013, passim

20. Max Dvorak, 1874-1921, Czech-born Austrian art historian

Leo Frobenius, 1873-1938, German ethnologist and archaeologist; founded the Institute for Cultural Morphology in Munich in 1920.

Alois Riegl, 1858-1905, Austrian art historian, interested in style and cultural history.

Georg Simmel, 1858-1918, German sociologist, philosopher and critic.

Wilhelm Worringer, 1881-1965, German art historian.

Heinrich Wölfflin, 1864-1945, Swiss aesthetician and art historian.

21. *The Trilogy of Culture*, p. 8.

22. 'The Metaphysical Meaning of Culture', in *The Trilogy of Culture*, p. 454.

Chapter 2

From *Philosophical self-presentation* (1938): A lecture delivered at the University of Cluj

We begin with extracts from the manuscript of the Conference on Blaga's self-presentation. This text clearly shows that in Blaga's philosophical works there is a systematic architectonics nor symphonic structure like that of a Byzantine church with many cupolas. His metaphysical construction does not erect one single idea but principal leit-motifs which interweave and return from one study to another in rhythmical alternation. In the Trilogies, the ideas set forth in the first volumes of each are crowned by a metaphysical perspective in the third. Blaga clearly expresses his appreciation of his principal achievement, with roots deep in his poetry and philosophy, a metaphysical representation of knowledge created **sub specie mysterii.**

The six systematic studies published so far complete each other and display a certain architectural vision. They are part of a more comprehensive approach that I hope to carry out through the years to come. All the six approaches belong to the same wider philosophical framework, and they finally outline a metaphysical vision of the whole of existence. Let me say a few words upon the architecture of this system. The system I am conceiving has, unlike the classical ones, a symphonic nature, being neither a one-idea-system, or a one-formula-system, but is structured rather like a multi-cupola church. Some principal, rhythmically alternating leitmotifs interweave in this system, which was conceived cyclically, in 'trilogies' dedicated to one group of daily experiences. Two of these 'trilogies' are already completed and published:

1.*The Trilogy of Knowledge*, containing: *The Dogmatic Aeon, Luciferian Knowledge, Transcendental Censorship;*

2. *The Trilogy of Culture*, containing: *Horizon and Style, The Mioritic Space, The Genesis of Metaphor and the Meaning of Culture*

I am presently working at *The Trilogy of Values* and the first version of Volume I, *Art and Value* is already completed. A volume on the 'equivalences of truth' and one dedicated to ethical issues are to appear in the same trilogy. Maybe I should not speak about works I have not written yet, but it might be worth presenting the framework of the trilogies already published. I shall only add that two other trilogies are going to be dedicated to some issues of the philosophy of biology and of pure metaphysics.

A central idea, supported by some other leitmotifs, certainly exists in the two trilogies that are already completed: it is the idea of 'mystery', of our existence in the horizon of mystery. Because the idea of mystery has such a central position, there have been voices criticising me for mysticism and, although I do not believe this would be a crime, I should state that I am not mystical in my philosophy. I may be in poetry or drama, where mystical experience has its place—that, I believe, no modern aesthetician can deny. However, my idea to place mystery in a central position of my philosophy is the consequence of the desire I have for a supreme position and exactness in my philosophical thinking. Thus, in *The Dogmatic Aeon* and *Luciferian Knowledge*, for the first time in the history of philosophy I thoroughly analysed and examined the very idea of mystery. Neither the philosophers, nor the theorists of science, have ever done this before. The issue of 'mystery' has been approached as vaguely as possible. I am the first who has ever tried to establish the role of this idea in the formative process of human knowledge. I tried, in *The Dogmatic Aeon* and *Luciferian Knowledge*, to provide a sort of logical, almost mathematical, analysis of the idea of mystery and after I placed it in a certain system of coordinates, I pointed out possible 'variants' of the idea of mystery. Those listeners who have not had the opportunity to read these studies, should not be alarmed by purely symbolical titles, such as *Luciferian Knowledge*. I assure them that we're not talking about the Devil: we're just trying to solve some issues concerning logic and the theory of knowledge: 'The Mystery' exists in our vision as a primary, irreducible horizon of our existence. This mystery is atomised, under the pressure and operations of the process of knowledge, into innumerable 'variants' that may be logically determined, as 'mysteries'. Here are some 'variants': first of all, there is the 'mystery' as the primary horizon of the human way of being. There is the 'mystery' that our senses report to us, a mystery described by signs by our empirical sensitivity; and then, the 'mystery revealed' in the constructive plane of our knowledge, on that of our imagination and that of abstract visions. This revealed-imaginary mystery may be described as it is and may be subject to a new 'revelation' The process may continue for ever. And the fact that the mystery may never be converted into non-mystery is also pointed out in my studies. Kant's 'thing in itself' is referred to in these studies as being one of the countless variants of the idea of mystery.

The analysis of the idea of mystery led me to some very peculiar variants. I am speaking about the 'intensified' or 'essentialised' mystery. These mysteries may be expressed and formulated only through antinomies, precisely through transfigured antinomies. In order to illustrate this idea of intensified, essentialised mystery, we refer to examples from Neo-Platonic metaphysics or from Christian theology. And this is a point on which I'd like to insist for a moment. I tried to point out that, as for the variants of the intensified, essentialised mystery, which may be expressed only by means of antinomy, a kind of knowledge is possible that has not been experienced since Neo-Platonic times and even since Christian dogmatics. I must specify that it is not the very content of the dogma that I wish to update, but the method that might be thence inferred, a method that may be updated and assimilated by philosophy, as for some external issues. On the other hand, it is worth observing that, due to quantum theory, modern physics states the antinomic structure of light; the phenomenon of light is perceived as being an 'undulation' as well as something 'corpuscular', which is a logically incomprehensible paradox. Still, some experiences necessarily demand this antinomic solution. This is why the belief is that modern physics is subject to a crisis. I believe that I succeeded in demonstrating that, as this undulatory-corpuscular theory of the nature of light is actually part of a *sui-generis* type of knowledge, which I called 'minus-knowledge', it is not a crisis of modern physics but a new type of knowledge that we're dealing with. We already know that Kant built a theory of knowledge that was actually meant philosophically to justify Newton's classical physics. Today Newton's physics represents only a limiting case for modern physics. Thus, the necessity for philosophically justifying the constructions of modern physics by means of a new theory of knowledge, is imperative. This is, essentially, what I tried to do in *The Dogmatic Aeon* and *Luciferian Knowledge*, especially by providing the theory of knowledge with the concept of 'direction'. Knowledge has not, as has been thought since

Kant, a unique sense ('plus'): to 'attenuate' mystery by means of an infinite theoretical process; knowledge has two opposite senses, namely, plus and minus. And there are circumstances when the 'minus' direction, that does not attenuate a mystery but, on the contrary, intensifies and radicalises it, rendering its formulating exclusively antinomic, is required. This is how modern physics acts in certain circumstances. These theories must not be regarded as an impasse, but, on the contrary, they justify a certain type of knowledge, that we have called 'minus-knowledge'. I shall have myself the opportunity to apply in some essential matters this method of minus-knowledge, that I have tried to justify for building a new theory of knowledge. My researches in this field conducted me to the discovery of some fundamental aspects of human knowledge, that remained unobserved until now. To my regret, I do not have the necessary time to present step by step the way I proceeded to this discovery. Thus, I restrict myself to some results. Knowledge has a dual nature, and this dualism is essential, irreducible to a common denominator: (1) the knowledge built within the frame of the given world and which can be completed with simple 'unknown factors', and (2) the knowledge built within the frame of mystery, where everything that can be referred to as belonging to the given world is only a sign or signalisation, via the senses, of certain mysteries. We called the first type of knowledge 'paradisiac' and the second one, 'Luciferian'. Within the framework of paradisaic knowledge, the idea of mystery, which is very complex, has no role, though, even in this framework of knowledge—which operates with intuitions, concepts and intellectual categories as they have been examined since Kant—there may be so-called 'unknown factors'. But mystery implies a more complex 'unknown factor'. Mystery and the attempt to reveal it are the object and task of Luciferian knowledge, which has *sui-generis* articulations and structures. All the elements that also have a role in paradisaic knowledge—experience, intuition, concept, categories—have different functions in the two types of knowledge. All of the theories of knowledge elaborated until now have attempted to reduce human knowledge to aspects related only to paradisaic knowledge. When I see a tree and I say, 'This tree is an apple tree' (even if I am the victim of an illusion), I perform an act of paradisaic knowledge. When I see the curtain in the window waving and I say, 'Something unknown', the X that produces the movement may be the wind, I also perform an act of paradisaic knowledge. However when I state 'light is an undulation', I perform an act of Luciferian knowledge. The light was first turned into a sensitive sign of the mystery, that we try to reveal to ourselves. The revealing of the unknown factor is in a certain way a *substitute* for the sensitive sign and it acquires a firmer existential value than the one the 'sign' is endowed with. The unknown does not approach the known at the same level as it does in paradisaic knowledge; on the contrary, once it is *revealed*, it becomes a *substitute* for the known.

Thus, all the aspects of Luciferian knowledge are essentially different from those of paradisaic knowledge:

Paradisaic knowledge / Luciferian knowledge:

'The mystery' is set forth and 'changed' by Luciferian knowledge through infinite processes of attenuation and perpetuation. All these aspects have nothing to do with paradisaic knowledge. Another result of my researches is that mystery can never be converted into non-mystery.

The third volume of the *Trilogy of Cognition*, that is *Transcendent Censorship*, which I called a metaphysical attempt, is a study that entirely differs from The *Dogmatic Aeon* and *Luciferian Knowledge*. I believe that I do not need to justify metaphysics at Cluj University, where there are so many brilliant teachers of philosophy. I just want to point out that metaphysics is different from science and even different from the philosophy of science. Metaphysics is always a leap into the uncontrollable. To put it this way: experience has just a 'veto' role in metaphysics, if the latter happens to contradict it. But experience should not control and verify—not in a positive way—metaphysical conceptions. I reflected upon the result acquired in the two preceding studies, that is the non-convertibility of mystery into non-mystery. I asked myself if this situation that we are doomed to bear does not have a metaphysical transcendent meaning. This was a metaphysical perspective. Suppose our individual consciousness, which includes knowledge and its possibilities and limits, is actually interrupted and controlled by a metaphysical centre, of a spiritual nature, but being above us. Let us call this spiritual centre *transcendent*, as for its relationship with our consciousness, 'The Great Anonym'. Admitting this metaphysical assumption, we could establish why man is not able to covert mystery in any positive or adequate manner. The Great Anonym imposes a censorship upon human knowledge, which prevents us—to our advantage—from knowing in an absolute manner, or from adequately revealing mysteries. This transcendent censorship applies to us structurally, by means of sensitive constants and intellectual categories, on which human knowledge perpetually depends. Intellectual categories would be the means of a transcendent censorship, that purposely and to our advantage and maybe to the advantage of the whole of existence, the Great Anonym uses in order to keep us away from mysteries. If we had the capacity of absolute knowledge, we would be endangered: we would cease our efforts or we would substitute ourselves for the Great Anonym, which would generate cosmic anarchy. We must therefore see the relativity of human knowledge not as a shortcoming, but as the result of a superior metaphysical order. This metaphysical conception of knowledge is in accordance with a given situation, the fact that mystery cannot be converted into non-mystery. It does not contradict the empirical results. Nevertheless, as it is a metaphysical conception, it cannot be controlled by means of empirical data. But this is a common place for every metaphysical conception. Anyway, my conception is the first attempt in recent times at a metaphysics of knowledge. It is absolutely new. And, as the author is a Romanian, I believe I have the right to claim that this metaphysical conception is Romanian too.

I shall now proceed further, to the second trilogy, which deals with another group of phenomena: cultural ones. Recent researches have increasingly highlighted the mental aspect of cultural phenomena, that is 'style'. It has been pointed out that there is a certain stylistic uniformity that is common for cultural phenomena: there is a same 'style' that applies to all cultural creations belonging to a certain space and time. Once stated, this stylistic aspect has generated increasing and assiduous debate, not only among art historians and critics, but also among philosophers of culture. However, the phenomenon of style demands an explanatory theory. This explanatory theory has gradually appeared: the first explanation, without a precise awareness of what they were dealing with, can be found in Classicism. To give an example, the great poet Hölderlin, who also was a greater thinker than he is believed to be, when attempting a determination of Greek style (the term was not used with its present meaning), used to speak about the popularity of the 'organic' vs. 'inorganic', which correspond approximately to Nietzsche's 'Apollonian' vs. 'Dionysian'. As a matter of fact, this latter pair of terms was also used by the Schlegel brothers in their approach to the Greek phenomenon, much before Nietzsche, but certainly not having the same visionary scope as the latter. Nietzsche as well as Simmel, Frobenius and Spengler, and then, more related to artistic phenomena, Alois Riegl, Worringer, Wölfflin and many others have tried to offer an explanatory theory of 'style'. As I showed in *The Trilogy of Culture*, all of them incline towards visualising 'style' as a 'monolithic' phenomenon, as I call it, and towards reducing it to a single factor, by hypostasising it. Frobenius' and Spengler's morphology approaches 'culture' as a unitary stylistic phenomenon, as a result of a soul of the culture, which rises as a spatial organism in a certain type of landscape and nowhere else. Culture, style, is supposed to be a parasitic organism, superimposed on the emotional life of man, and is supposed to have every characteristic of a genuine organism: it is born, it grows and dies. The lifetime of a culture, that has a monadic nature is, according to Spengler, around 800-1000 years. Each culture or cultural style is dominated by a certain feeling of the space connected to a certain landscape. I thoroughly examined these theories in The *Trilogy of Culture*, where I also proposed a new explanatory theory of cultural style, a theory that, in our opinion, overcomes all the difficulties which face all other existing theories. We explain cultural style by means of categories of the unconsciousness. We have already pointed out that it is not only our consciousness that has its own series of cognitive 'categories' meant to receive data from the world. We admit that, beyond these categories of knowledge, about which philosophers have been speaking since Aristotle, and especially since Kant, there is a second-wide series of categories of the unconsciousness, categories that we call, because of their depth and to their place, 'abyssal'. There certainly is a correspondence between the categories of conscious knowledge and these abyssal categories of the unconsciousness, but the latter have a different structure. Admitting that our consciousness has, as a form or category of sensitivity, 'space' and the 'time', we admit that our unconscious also has its own space and time, only that they have a different structure. To the unconscious expressed in Western culture we assign a category of infinite tri-dimensional space, while to the unconscious expressed in our Romanian culture we assign an undular space. We find a certain temporal form expressed in Western culture, that is, ascending time, the basin-time, as we called it. But as for the ancient times, especially with regard to the Hellenic culture, we found another shape of time, cascade-time. We cannot justify this theory with all the necessary examples, but they can be found in the three volumes of the *Trilogy of Culture*. There also is, in our unconscious, another category besides space and time, the formative category which tends to individualisation, typification or elementarisation. The unconscious also includes the category of 'expansion' or 'withdrawal' from the stylistic horizon. In what he creates, the European, for example, is generally dominated by the category of 'expansion', while the Indian is dominated by the category of 'withdrawal'. But, as I was saying, our unconscious has many heterogeneous categories, all of them converging to create a *stylistic universe*. All cultural creations, e., works of art, metaphysical visions, great scientific theories, mythology and others, are marked by the existence of their abyssal categories, which are connected, by a para-correspondence, with the respective conscious categories, but are differently structured. This not a new 'categorical' theory because nobody ever thought to establish these categories, but because it has the advantage of explaining—in a more satisfactory manner than others—the multiplicity and variability of the aspects of stylistic phenomenon. We do not study 'style' as monolithic phenomenon but as a complex phenomenon that is sustained by an entire complex of heterogeneous 'abyssal categories', and by a cosmic-genetic synergy. This has also the importance of highlighting, for the first time, certain aspects of the 'unconscious'.

Beyond its general theoretical advantages, this categorical theory of the basis of stylistic phenomenon provides us with the possibility of examining stylistically—for the first time and more thoroughly—our folk culture. My study *Mioritic Space* has been a best-seller among all my studies. In this study, my point was to demonstrate the existence of a series of abyssal categories, effectively active in our people's creations. Therefore, I discovered in the *doina* song the undular space, the same valley/hill horizon which I could distinguish in the sentiment of destiny that is typical of our lyrical poetry, that expresses the Romanian way. I pointed out the importance of the 'sophianic' category, in our culture and the importance of the descending transcendent, of the 'organic' category for the entire spiritual life of the South-East Europeans. I also showed the efficacy of the 'ghostly', or elementarising category for folk art. And so on. I believe this is enough to provide an understanding of the efficiency of our theory upon style. As a matter of fact, I gladly observe that most of our younger literary critics successfully applied these ideals in many areas as well as in monographic studies. Thus, the data provided to supply a stronger basis to our theory becomes more and more impressive. Anyway, this theory has cleared the way for new approaches, general as well as specific, that have finally begun to show their efficacy.

After elaborating the theory of abyssal categories, which I was the only one to have discovered, I had to make this theory of 'culture' and 'style' become part of the metaphysic system I am working at. I did this in *The Genesis of Metaphor and the Meaning of Culture*. In this recent study, I worked upon a metaphysical anthropology and a metaphysical theory of the meaning of culture and style. It is the first attempt that has been made in philosophy to elaborate a metaphysics of stylistic phenomena. 'Metaphor' and 'style' are the fundamentals of any cultural creation. Any such creation is an attempt of man to reveal mystery to himself. But this revelation, whether realised by artistic, theoretical or visionary creation, always has a metaphorical nature in its constitution, and is made with stylistic co-ordinates and forms. This means that revelation of mystery is never adequate. Not only human knowledge of the ineffable world, but also our attempts to reveal mysteries by means of creations are subject to a transcendent censorship. The categories that form the basis of a certain style are given to us as transcendent hindrances; this is how the Great Anonym prevents us from revealing mysteries in a positive way and with accurate adequacy, lest we should attempt to substitute ourselves for him and disturb the cosmic balance, but it also is to our advantage, in order to preserve our permanent creative state and protect us from the unknown dangers of absolute revelation. Man has, unlike animals, a specific way of being: it is living within the horizon of mystery, aiming to reveal it. But our revelations are just metaphors of mystery and their transcendence is limited by the censorship of abyssal categories.

Translated by Angela Crocus

Chapter 3

From *The Dogmatic Aeon* (1931)

From 'The Dogmatic Aeon'

The eschatological feeling of the end of the world and of the beginning of a new spiritual aeon, present in **The Dogmatic Aeon**, *seems to us to be the generating motive of the whole of Blaga's philosophy, receptive to the new spiritual epoch and also creating it. Contemporary commentators on the ideas of* **The Dogmatic Aeon** *explain that Blaga was well attuned by such concepts to the specific cultural paradigms which have appeared in recent decades. He put into relief the similarities between our epoch and the Hellenistic, both producers of aeons ('new spiritual worlds of long duration') and certain aspirations to syntheses, combinations of Asiatic with European thought, gropings for the meanings of worlds under disparate and diverse appearances, the existence of a doctrine that combines religious visions, Asiatic and Christian, with scientific and philosophical ideas, hybridisations of the abstract with the mythological, gropings after morphological correspondences of different zones of the universe under forms of 'typical configurations', the foundations of a new ontology and a reformed theory of knowledge which leads to relativism and desire for a philosophy of history.*

Our concluding considerations do not follow necessarily from the preceding ones. We arrive at the drafting table where perspectives are pioneered. And perspectives cling to vision rather than syllogism. Because the first link of our analyses is made up of several historical observations, we should also conclude with a few historical considerations. It has been observed that our examination of dogma has not been done exclusively for its own sake. If we had not anticipated a huge potential for actualisation, the issue would have been of little interest to us. The motive behind our examination is circumscribed by our strong interest in the questions of our current historical moment.

In the chapters devoted to the structure and justification of dogma, we presented the inner make-up of dogmatic thinking, and an attempt to justify it within the bounds of cognition. We saw how at times a given set of data, intersecting with the logical lines, pushes the intellect to ecstasy. In conclusion, we will briefly approach the issue from another angle.

Considerations of a different nature, that do not fall under the theory of knowledge or logic, but under the philosophy of culture or the philosophy of history, make us believe that the historical rhythm itself leads us to affirm intellectual ecstasy as a possible mode of cognition for a whole age. Certainly, not that the mode of cognition of the future will be ecstatic in every moment and in all circumstances, but simply that the future will resort to ecstatic thinking *in extremis* alongside ordinary thinking—which has not happened in the history of the European spirit since the crystallisation of Christian dogma. From a historical perspective, the dogmatic has always been understood as reactionary, but in this study we gave it a renewing purport, that of an initiative, of a new beginning.

In the Introduction we presented dogma as a creative solution for the great Hellenistic crisis. If we were to search the past for an age in which the contours of our age are reflected, as in a mirror, we would encounter only one such age: the Hellenistic. What does the similarity consist of, heretofore not unnoticed, between the present and the Hellenistic ages?

At least as a parenthesis, permit us to point out that the increasing number of studies published in the last few years on various Hellenistic aspects and moments—on the mind, art and ethos of that age—seems to be extremely symptomatic. Perhaps not without good reason, we perceive a sympathy between the two ages in this increased interest in Hellenism, a sympathy based on their kinship. However, this fact constitutes only a symptom. The real similarities between the two ages must be traced on the contours of the face in the mirror.

The aspiration for syntheses is kindled in an impressive manner, and is a mark of the times. The extraordinary abundance of doctrines promising a universal cure for the spiritual crisis of the age is the same as in the Hellenistic period. Never in historical memory have the Asian and the European minds clashed and mingled with each other, aspiring with the same thrilling persuasion towards a mutual understanding or towards a superior amalgam, as both today and during the spiritual empire of Alexander. In the history of Europe, as well as in the history of Asia, numerous efforts have been made toward larger syntheses, but never have the cosmic conceptions been built on more diverse foundations, and, if you please, with such disparate elements as in our time and in the centuries that preceded the Christian era. We live in a strange atmosphere, with signs that need to be interpreted and analogies that carry thinking further. It is significant that some ideas and modes belonging to Hellenism, and which lay forgotten for 2000 years, are brought up again, having a mysterious grip on the modern mind. The late Stoic philosophers and various Gnostic schools discovered that the conceptions about the world of various peoples hide, under eternally different aspects, the same *meaning*, and that the important thing is *the meaning*, not the cover. Myths, cultures were reduced by the Gnostics to explanations with similar content. The present is searching for the same deeper meaning, hidden behind a variety of cosmic conceptions from all over the world. The emergence of thinkers curiously researching all the doctrines of the Earth, especially Asian ones, wears the seal 'Hellenistic.' What else are, for instance, the anthroposophy of Rudolf Steiner or the heavy spiritualism of Keyserling, if not syntheses of the Asian and Christian doctrines, modern science and philosophy? Owing to their complex, layered character, Steiner's anthroposophy or Keyserlingian spiritualism, to mention just a few well-known attempts, are possible only in a Hellenistic type of historical framework. The similarities between the Hellenistic period and the present time occur both in the contents of thought and in the style of thinking. A series of newer thinkers wants to build bridges to reach the ultimate meaning of existence, using terms and visions from mythology similarly to the Gnostic thinkers, in a manner both realistic and symbolic at the same time. Contemporary abstract thinking is contaminated by myth. The thinkers advocating the common good mix, in the bundle of yarn from which they spin their systems, the silk of abstraction, the yarn remnants of experience and the unqualified subject matter of clairvoyant knowledge. While not similar in content, notice the similarity in the manner in which contemporary philosophy uses terms such as 'Apollonian', 'Faustian', 'demoniac', and the use of mythological elements in all Gnostic systems (in which likewise the various deities represent abstract essences). In both cases, the thinker is situated between abstraction and myth. Without difficulty a kinship could also be established between the symbolist-allegorical method so current in Gnostic thinking and the method of the same sort at home in modern psychoanalysis: 'the far-off analogy,' cultivated with eager interest both then and now. For instance, Simon Magus said that the Biblical text about man's life in Paradise must be interpreted in view of the fact that the paradise is nothing but man's intrauterine existence. (Leisegang, *Die Gnosis*, Alfred Kröner Verlag, 1924, page 75.) This is an example of the extent to which the Gnostics would go to build symbolic analogies. If we read the interpretations of the myths written by a contemporary psychoanalyst, we would encounter identical exegeses.

The triumphant entry of ideas such as 'configuration' into science, psychology, biology and physics, can be a suggestive reason for comparing the two epochs. Rightly amazed, we currently witness the renaissance of the magic sciences about the hidden correlations in the universe and of the morphological ones which seek to guess the whole by studying the details. The Gnostic thinking also moved between 'forms' and 'correlations.' To accept the fundamental and irreducible existence of a 'configuration' in various domains, as our time does, means to open the gate for the most diverse preoccupations considered until recently at least without any scientific foundation, if not superstitious. We would not be surprised at all if we witnessed astrology taking back its official function, based on a philosophy of configuration and correlations. This prediction is repeated yet more often; we record it as a symptom without passing any judgment whatsoever on the justification of such 'sciences'.

The troubling interest in the occult phenomena is one of the most striking common traits of the two epochs which preoccupy us. As a curious note, it should be remembered that the old esoteric schools knew the living mechanism of the occult phenomena and often described theogonic or cosmogonic processes as phenomena of meta-psychic materialisation.

As far as today's purely philosophical currents are concerned, they are relativistic, as in the Hellenistic period. Scepticism ruled then; pragmatism and fiction rule today. The disillusioned intellect cannot muster the strength to believe in the objectivity of its own fabrications; and it is content that this idea, which can be replaced with a whole swarm of other ideas, for a moment gives it the opportunity to enjoy the free play of its functions. This circumstance, namely philosophy's discouraging nature, facilitated to a great extent, in the old days as well as today, the invasion of vision and myth into philosophy. This in turn led to the formations of the Gnostic metaphysics, at the same time barbarian and refined—with kindred appearances in our time.

Add to these similarities the strong attraction toward philosophy of history. Hellenistic and modern thinkers alike wonder about the meaning of various cultures, about the purpose or direction of history. While bitter for some, and a heavenly hope for others, emphasis is placed on the fatality of history. Then, as well as today, existed a distinct feeling that something was going to end and something new would begin. This feeling of an ending and of a beginning is not the feeling of an insignificant ending and an insignificant beginning. It is an eschatological feeling of the end of the world and an aeonic feeling of the beginning of a new world.

The Ancients understood 'aeons' as long historical periods, universal times. 'Aeon' means to us a new spiritual world lasting a very long time. In history, we can distinguish two kinds of periods. There are periods of local cultures, of particular aspects, encircled within themselves, whose horizon is fatally narrow; they are attached to certain exclusive forms of life and thinking, endowed with lively mobility, but swapping among a limited number of creation motifs. And there are the aeonic periods. The aeonic periods are characterised by an enormous development of conscience; they are unhindered by the temporal-spatial environment. Their generating centre clings to the spiritual stratosphere. They have the tendency to go beyond any horizon. Their dominant characteristic is not particularism, but their *universal aspirations*. These are periods of vast syntheses, when life is run from a spiritual centre. Examples of such aeonic periods are Buddhism for Asia, and the Christian church for our world. The passing from a period of local cultures to an aeonic one does not occur without serious spiritual and intellectual crises. Hellenism was such a crisis of passing from an era of local cultures to an era of intense and monumental spiritualism (the Christian aeon, approximately the first 1,000 years of our era). After the Romano-German impact on history as well as that of the Slavs, a new period of local cultures developed on the Christian foundation (approximately the second millennium of our era). We experience today a crisis of passing from this cultural period to a new aeon. The spiritual crisis of our time is 'Hellenistic', and has many aspects that can be regarded as both advantages and disadvantages: the heterogeneous mixing of doctrines yet unstructured into a whole, the relativisation of philosophy, the attack of the mythical on the consciousness of our time, the timid emergence of a new visionary ontology, the thirst for ultimate syntheses and the tragic incapacity of the intellect to create such syntheses. Through all its elements melting together in its witches' chaldron, ancient Hellenism led eventually to a vertical change, elevating life an octave higher on the scale of spiritualism; in a similar manner, modern 'Hellenism' will lead to a new anchoring of life to the spiritual and to a comparable vertical change in depth and in height. This change interests us only from an intellectual point of view and, from this angle, the spiritual will suffer the passage from the enstatic intellect to the ecstatic intellect. Naturally, the Christian aeon can only provide a vague analogy to what the new aeon will be. We doubt that historical analogy has the principled significance accorded by some thinkers; yet because of the profound and obvious similarities between our time and Hellenism, the emergence of a new dogmatic aeon can be predicted with enough accuracy, as in the past, a spiritual aeon which, as far as thinking is concerned, will get its creative impulses from an initial rehabilitation of the ecstatic intellect, despite all risks involved in it.

Some of the élite thinkers of our time give us valuable clarifications about the change underway, but very little about its perspectives. Spengler announced years ago his eschatological feeling about the end of the European culture—it is true, in a wholly naturalistic sense. The aeonic feeling did not clasp him. Concomitant with this foreboding of collapse, other voices were heard, voices of urging and of hope. After fathoming the waters of the spirit from everywhere, as a stalwart condottiere of the idea, Keyserling believes in life's elevation to a new spiritual height. Nonetheless, he is as far from the concept of a new dogmatic aeon as are all species of rationalist thinkers, though he deservedly surpasses them. Berdyaev, feeding on the depth of the Russian steppe, forewarns of the new Middle Ages. Undoubtedly, to a great extent, Berdyaev's thinking is permeated by an aeonic feeling. As a necessary part of a theological conception of history, 'The New Middle Ages' is more a restoration than a creation. The New Middle Ages would develop as a religious flora grown under the sun of Christian dogma, and as an unit of social forms having in their centre the Christian church. Berdyaev sees the new age as the Middle Ages are viewed traditionally, anti-historical. His conception is romantic. Forever clinging to the past,

Berdyaev sees dogma from a faith perspective, as something global. He does not sublimate it. For that reason, he could not rise to the idea that is fundamental in our view, namely the ecstatic intellect destined to create new philosophical dogmas—a metaphysics in accordance with the inherent tendencies of the time. According to Berdyaev, history is used up, finished, bankrupt; the only salvation, he believes, is re-entry under the roof of the Christian faith, which man exited through trial and temptation. We believe only in an historical crisis (which we have called Hellenistic); in the oven of this crisis, at a very high temperature, the bricks for the new building are being made. We imagine the dogmatic aeon possessing all virtues of novelty; at its gates we knock. We do not see how elements of specific Christian dogma (out-of-date as regarding content) can enter. For the time being, the only similar characteristic between the Christian aeon and the new aeon we see being developed is the forms, or the style of ecstatic intellect. This available *ecstatic intellect* will take its material, which will be transfigured into new dogmas, from the fretting consciousness of the time, not from antique museums.

The demand for thinkers is to co-operate. If we were to take into account the contrasting rhythm of historical periods, we could argue that individualism is agonisingly experiencing its last excesses, so that tomorrow's metaphysics will probably no longer be the metaphysics of one individual or another, nor a vanishing expression of the personality of thinkers at odds with one another because of embarrassing tendencies to individualistic atomisation, but a metaphysics built little by little in a continuous process, marked by adventures, defeats and victories, and by the work of several generations under the sign of the ecstatic intellect.

The other angles and aspects of the still opaque crystal of the aeon, whose first signs we discern, is a matter of research. Will the future also witness the re-editing of the dogmatic as constraint? We ask this question with the necessary hesitation, but being fully aware that the future can close within itself every possible surprise. No matter how difficult to understand is this today, the historical rhythm does not exclude the emergence of a constraining factor at a spiritual level which will endow the new dogmas, once fully crystallised, with that *usual* meaning of dogmatic, namely the aura of immutability. But even the possible stabilisation of the new dogmas by coercive measures will not be final because history knows not finality. We tend to think, anyway, that the new metaphysics will be based not only on abstract concepts, but also on the creation of a new mythical thinking. The emergence of a new religious spirit, which will make human personality serve the dogma of tomorrow, seems more than natural to us. It is not impossible that the ethos would be based on anonymous stylising, and that the cult of the individual would become completely obsolete, for a while. The future is the realm of dreams; and for the time being, we can dream a lot, unpunished.

Translated by Monica Voiculescu and Delia Ursulescu

Chapter 4

From *The Divine Differentials* (1940)

(A) From 'The Great Anonym, the Generator'

Blaga presents an original cosmology in which the 'Great Anonym' (his equivalent to the One, God, the Absolute, in other systems) does not create, nor fashions a co-existing matter, nor is the source of successive but diminishing emanations, but inhibits its own self-reproducing tendency, which would otherwise result in the cosmic anarchy of a multitude of co-equal Gods. Instead, it directly produces 'divine differentials', simple structures from its own substance which form the ultimate constituents of the empirical world, and thus indirectly produces the complex structures formed from them. One complex structure is man, who, if he could attain absolute knowledge would therefore threaten the Great Anonym as a co-equal and thus would open up again the possibility of cosmic anarchy. Therefore man's knowledge is limited by the Great Anonym's 'transcendental censorship', the theme of the book of that name, so that man always comes up against mysteries which he can never fully comprehend. Blaga's cosmology thus provides a metaphysical explanation of one aspect of his epistemology. As Blaga makes clear in this passage and the next, he holds that metaphysics is free, speculative construction which goes beyond experience, though it can be falsified by it, yet needs to be self-consistent, and that therefore it is fundamentally in the same position as theorising in science. That we do in fact live and think on the level of mystery, that is, in a world which always outruns our comprehension of it, thus confirms Blaga's metaphysics but, even in his own eyes, cannot prove it.

We cannot speak about a genesis of the world without admitting the existence of a metaphysical centre, which is something else than the world. We have tried, in a few previous works, to outline this thought regarding a 'metaphysical centre' of existence. Certainly, the idea has been long acknowledged now, but it allows for progressive outlines. Looking for a name for that overwhelming yet hardly fathomed centre, we have reached the conclusion that we have to make use of a term meant firstly to keep awake our capacity of bewilderment and guessing. We have started our journey by calling him: the Great Anonym. The term, even though it may not have a demonstrative value, to the designated existence it includes all that our soul may offer to this pre-sensed existence, beyond any light and any darkness, that is all submission and bewilderment. The Great Anonym is the existence that keeps us on the outskirts, that turns us down, that puts barriers in front of us, but to which any other existence is indebted. Travelling inside ourselves, while seeking for him, we have, at a certain moment, imagined him beyond ourselves as well. Then, we have had to think him with his displaced accent and weight ever farther from us, in zones above all being. Readers may recall that, sometimes, we have had doubts whether we should call the Great Anonym, 'God'. Our hesitation is pardonable, because the Great Anonym baffles us by his egocentric habits and by his making use of certain measures, whose prompt qualification would bring about the theologians' awe. The Great Anonym, while turning away from what to us is the supreme principle of behaviour, defends himself not only against our justified curiosity, but also against our high assertion that we see it as a sacred duty. We shall see in this study that the Great Antonym's egocentricity exceeds by far what we have shown above. We have to admit that, in order to judge such a situation, we do not have at our disposal only very fragile and, particularly, very human criteria. Metaphysics should not be blamed because it sometimes makes use of strong words. Actually, it does not act ostentatiously. The strong word is rather the sign of astonishment in front of this dilemma. But theologians, neither, have serious reasons for such a fright, because the aspects that give the impression that we would live on the periphery of a demoniac foundation, allow for a rehabilitation, at a different level. The Great Anonym takes preventive measures so that man, and creatures in general, should not be able to assert themselves except within certain limits. Everything takes place as if the creature might, were it not for the preventive measures, become a threat to the Great Anonym. If we question the legitimacy of the preventive measures and interdictions under discussion, we shall not hesitate for one second to admit that they are fully justified not only from the angle of the anonymous centralism but also from that of the cosmic balance. In this way, we come, while making a detour, to bestow divine attributes on the Great Anonym, which, in the absence of the necessary perspective, we could not have decided to do. Were we to give the word a more a elastic sense than usual, nothing would stop us any longer from calling the Great Anonym

'God'. All the more so as, beyond the Great Anonym, we cannot see, much as we would squint our eyes, a more central existence.

The Great Anonym is a 'unitary entity' of an utmost substantial and structural complexity, a wholly autarchic existence, namely a self-sufficient one. Being fully aware that we are suggesting a metaphysical myth, we assign the Great Anonym the ability of 'self-reproducing' himself *ad infinitum*, in an identical way, without exhausting and without assimilating outward substances. With this we have outlined the thesis that we mean to place at the foundation of our speculative enterprise. There is here a fundamental proposition that we intend to put to trial. It does not claim to be a dogma, in the usual sense of the word, nor a supreme result of certain inductions. It represents only an anticipation that can ask for the reader's consent only progressively, and to the extent to which it will be able to organise a metaphysical outlook of wide scope, without entering into conflict with the results of experience. Nor do we want our initial proposition be accompanied by that apparently stringent way of argumentation, otherwise ambiguous and full of holes, that the pre- and post-Kantian metaphysics excessively used with so much naiveté. That way of argumentation, while operating with ambiguous and limited notions, can enjoy the value of a setting only within a truly architectonic and constructive metaphysical system. And we can do very well without such a setting. Our basic proposition is not meant to feed other vain hopes, either. One should not expect from us, for instance, a discourse, as much erudite as inconsistent, about the 'infinite' and 'absolute' attributes of the Great Anonym. We do not mean in the least to follow the example of classical metaphysics which, giving in to temptation, plunged into the game of unavoidable antinomies. With notions such as 'the infinite' or 'the absolute', which particularly flourish in the uncertain region of speculation, one can beat about the bush forever, but one cannot hope to build a metaphysics likely to be of use today. For instance, speaking about the Great Anonym's 'might', we shall avoid saying that it is 'absolute', as if one could not conceive of a greater one. This might is 'absolute' only in the sense of a superlative reality, that is, in the sense that it is thoroughly overwhelming as compared to the creature's powers. Therefore, we should not like the words about the Great Anonym to be given too rigid a significance. Here, usually, words represent metaphorical superlatives, seen from a human angle, in a perspective that thoroughly exceeds the creature's proportions. Therefore, in keeping with his complexity and plenitude, we assign the Great Anonym the ability to 'generate' an unlimited number of identical existences. Resolving to take into consideration only the Great Anonym's disposition and natural abilities, we should say that he is not a creator of worlds, but a generator of equivalent Gods. The Great Anonym exists under the pressure of a task immanently his, whose natural issue would be an endless theogony. This is the first premise, which we shall analyse in due time from an epistemological viewpoint as an expression of a potential mystery, but which, for the time being, is but the point from which we launch the arrow. This premise, which we accept in awareness of its role in the process of precipitating a cosmic system, explicates our determination to understand everything, and the Great Anonym's 'plenitude' as being endowed with supreme abilities at the 'generating' level as well. The presupposed initial situation would allow for figuratively mathematical formulations, in terms that belong to calculation, but, as we have said earlier, we find it wiser to avoid any dialectics, which would be of interest only for beginners insofar as this problem is concerned. Let us resume the naked thesis so that we may step further. The Great Anonym, an existence of an overwhelming complexity and scope, possesses in himself, without being subject to any diminution or feeding, the ability to generate *ad infinitum* existences of the same substantial scope and the same structural complexity [as himself]. The Great Anonym represents a fully autarchic system; he exists as a self-sufficient entity, but, owing to his plenitude, he is directed towards a reproductive genesis. However, owing to some special measures, the Great Anonym's reproductive abilities remain an eternal virtuality, since the unleashing of the reproductive process would breed either other 'divine entities', that is as many autarchic systems which would elude the central watch and control, or some egocentric systems which would try to substitute themselves for the first and for all the others. In both cases, the result would be, in one way or another, a serious theo-anarchy. Thus, from the very beginning, the Great Anonym finds himself in a paradoxical impasse. What we have here is a impasse in point of perspective, a impasse previous to any derived, second-hand existence. The impasse is caused by that which might take place as well as by the need to avoid consequences equalling the disaster of existence. Reasons such as these regarding that impasse will decide the path the Great Anonym will take, because the Great Anonym does not abandon himself to a natural process, but takes a path ordered by superior considerations. It is at this moment that what we might call the

From The Divine Differentials (1940) 49

Great Anonym's 'will' starts operating, a will directed by the advice he gives himself. In order to prevent the theogonic process and its anarchic consequences, the Great Anonym will deliberately paralyse his reproductive abilities, and on a large scale at that. The Great Anonym is virtually a generator of 'divine entities' equal to himself, but, in order to save the centralism of existence, the Great Anonym will only make himself conspicuous through reproductive acts with a minimised objective; minimised both from a substantial and a structural viewpoint. These minimised reproductive acts are the so-called 'creative' acts of the divinity, which have often been, by analogy, compared to the 'work creative' acts of *man*. A painful and clumsy anthropomorphism has slipped into views of the Divinity's creative acts. Even though one cannot build a metaphysics in the absence of anthropomorphism, there is no doubt that their number must be cut to the minimum. The Great Anonym's creative acts are not acts creating something out of nothing, nor are they acts applied on a given material. The Great Anonym's acts are rather improperly called 'creative acts' since, in essence, they are *reproductive* acts. But not even an act of the Great Anonym does not declare itself, such as it might do, namely neither as an act of his nor as an explicit generator of a 'divine unit'. Given his global reproductive abilities, the Great Anonym intervenes with acts of preventive cancelling of a maximum extent: only in this way can the Great Anonym save the centralism of existence. The Great Anonym's *direct* 'creatures' are not, in other words, the result of a creative will proper, which would proceed to achieve 'substances' and 'forms' out of nothing; the *direct* creatures are the effect of some 'reproductive' act of Divinity, *left unsuspended from his will*. The Great Anonym's will, as an effort, is not directed towards creation but its objective is precisely the prevention of too large a generating scope. The divine will is but the substratum of a greatly ample eliminatory operation, or of a systematic *deterioration and decimation* of 'possibilities'. The primordial concern of the divinity is not 'creation', but the *prevention or extreme extinction of a possible theogonic process*. The positive permitted possibility of the Great Anonym's creative act together with the suspended possibilities would yield a 'divine entity'. That which allows itself to be 'created' and what is 'prevented' complete each other complementarily: these two parts would breed together a God, just as in physics two superposed complementary colours give white or sunlight. The assertion is perfectly legitimate according to which any undiscriminated possibility of the Great Anonym is the minor complement of an immense mass of suppressed possibilities; any direct creature of the Great Anonym will be a tiny fragment, allowed and freely accomplished by a possible God. We have repeated several times the expression about a *direct creation* of the Great Anonym. The given world (the cosmos) is, as we'll show later on, the result of a *direct* creation as regards the substratum-elements, but also of an *indirect* one in point of *complex* substances and forms. Actually, the Great Anonym creates the world both directly and indirectly, exclusively led by the will to prevent 'filiation'. In other words, the creation of the world has the aspect of a solution of the impasse. But it is the only solution, the optimum one. The possibility of *thorough*, endless reproduction lies in the very 'nature' of the Great Anonym; therefore the *real* creative act is only what remains uncensored after the check of the divinity's circumspect eye. The Great Anonym's will has no analogies with man's will, or, at least, it has a different meaning: it is not plainly creative or constructive, but definitely eliminatory. If *thorough* reproduction is the expression of divine *nature* itself, then the Great Anonym's will is *par excellence* a 'denaturing' ability. Any act of the Great Anonym must actually be considered as a denatured creation or procreation, until failure of recognition, through radical anticipated mutilation. 'Hypostases', if by this term we understand identical or similar existences, are the most natural possibilities of the Great Anonym, not two, nor three, but countless. Yet, the prospect of hypostases represents at the same time the great fear of the Anonymous Substance. God proceeds to create the world both directly and indirectly, because he fears the Son ever and ever again. God is 'theogonic' through his very *nature,* but, having to save the centralism of existence, he must needs become anti-theogonic. The Great Anonym, the generating plenitude itself, imposes, for superior reasons, a burning cruelty upon his *possibilities:* the endless theogonic filiation is replaced by reproductive acts previously rendered harmless through minimisation. Identical or similar existences: these form the second day's prospect of the divinity, since everything that is related to the Great Anonym is fully accomplished in himself. In him, we find in a state of possibility only repetition, reproduction; but '*exact'* reproduction would mean, through its consequences, a decentralisation, a theo-anarchy which worries the Great Anonym to such an extent that he will resort to severe, systematic, ruthless suppressions. We shall have the opportunity to see how much care is invested in this preventive

From The Divine Differentials (1940) 51

system, and how circumspectly, the inner God of all circles avoids the danger that threatens Him due to his own nature.

Since we have brought hypostases into discussion, that is, identical or similar existences, it is probably appropriate to clear up our position towards the systems that allow for the reality of hypostases. It is fairly well known that Neo-Platonism and various Gnostic outlooks admit either three or a whole series of hypostases of the supreme unity. The supreme unity, the one above any category, yields, according to Plotinus, a copy slightly inferior to itself: reason (*nous, logos*); and reason yields a further copy again slightly inferior to itself: the world's soul (Demiurge), who would be the world's maker following to certain Ideas, more remote copies, in their turn, of the divine reason. Things would take place according to the principle of encapsulated projectiles, and would look like a cascade through a channel of similarities. 'Decadence' would be inherent in hypostases, namely, a normal process since, finally, any emanation would *inevitably* be inferior to the source. However, the corruption of hypostases is not so serious as to be irremediable. According to the Neo-Platonists, man's mission is precisely that of climbing again the slope of cosmic decadence up to reunion with the supreme unity, an achievement reached sometimes in the so-called states of ecstasy. Cosmic decadence is regarded as a reversible process, as if everything took place, to the creature's relief, on a scale of approximate similitudes. *Nous*, reason, would be a copy of the divine unity, a not altogether perfect copy, but anyway a recognisable one, and the world's Soul would be a copy of Reason, again a not altogether perfect copy, but a copy nevertheless. The initial entity is to be found in less structured form in the entity that is Reason, and Reason is to be found in a less structured form in the entity that is the world's Soul. The *resemblance* between the model and the ensuing copy is overwhelmingly more important in comparison with the unessential corruption inevitably endured by the copy, and in certain cases, the copy can even restore its perfect resemblance to the model. We have a different outlook on the basic cosmogonic process. Any creative act (only improperly called so) of the Great Anonym is in respect of possibility, as we have asserted, an act of global procreation on his part, but, in respect of realisation, any such act is, for highly centralist reasons, deliberately *strangled* to the maximum. The disanalogy between the Great Anonym and any direct or indirect result of creative acts is overwhelming and irreversible, as compared to the similarity which is overshadowed by it, and is, in any case, negligible. That is why it seems that man's mission is entirely other than seeking to make himself the likeness of the one who had previously taken pains to mutilate him, and who, by all the preventive measures taken, tends precisely to preserve this disanalogy. The Great Anonym is the existence threatened by only one danger, the danger of its own identity-generating nature, but the Great Anonym is also the sole existence, which rescues everything through his ruthless will, directed by the negations of a hegemonic anticipation. 'The world' is not the result of a natural emanative process, but the sum total of the direct and indirect results of generating acts *purposely* suppressed or distorted *beyond recognition*. The objective of the Great Anonym's generating act has the complex scope of the divine entity, but this objective is always *deliberately* restricted to a segment absolutely simple in point of structure, and minimised to the maximum in point of substance. Such a result might be called: a '*divine differential*'. The Great Anonym's genetic acts therefore take place in terms opposite to the possible ones. We shall come to see the meaning of this spiteful genesis. For the time being, let us note that the sole results of the genesis are the divine differentials, and that any more complex creature is but the result of some indirect geneses, having as a basis the divine differentials themselves. The Great Anonym's generating possibilities, freely and uncontrollably unleashed, would breed an endless series of similar divine existences, huge mountains with the same altitude, among which would open ravines marking the generating rhythm. Such a genesis would end in the mountains' struggle to usurp the centre. For this reason, and for a few others, the Great Anonym decides for a genesis *rebours*, through 'differentials'. (. . .)

According to Leibniz, God is the creator of the 'world'. The world is made of numberless 'monads'. But each monad is an 'individual', a microcosm, which mirrors, more or less clearly, the world in its entirety. Leibniz states that there are not two monads identical to each other.

As compared to any emanational system, our system may be characterised as a deliberately differentiated and hegemonically adjusted reproductionism. This genesis is singular in its own way; it has no empirical model, unlike any emanational and creationist system.

The world's genesis would not have been started, had the Great Anonym abandoned himself unreservedly to his natural reproductive possibilities. In that case, there would have taken place

From The Divine Differentials (1940) 53

a genesis of systems evading the control of a centre and guided instead by the tendency towards mutual usurpation. Fortunately, the Great Anonym's generating plenitude also stands under the sign of precaution and will. However, the Great Anonym's will is not, like that of man's, a positively achieving ability, but firstly an ability in the service of a huge denial, the ability of distortion, of suspending possibilities on the verge of coming into being. The world, with its beings, and with man within it, is not owed to the Great Anonym in the sense of '*natura naturans*'; it is owed to the Great Anonym's reproductive abilities, distorted to the maximum according to hegemonic anticipations. The Great Anonym's volitional effort has as an objective *that which should not be done*, a *not what is being done*. Given God's reproductive abilities, what is to be wondered is not so much the creation of the world as the fact that the divine series [the theogonic process] is not born. If we manage to explain why the divine series is not being born, we clarify *eo ipso* the world's creation, since the *world is but the sediment of some radically and deliberately hindered theogonic processes*. In this order of ideas, the existence of the world appears as a proof that the Great Anonym has no other hypostases. The world came into existence on two levels: first, on the level of God's '*ad infinitum*' reproductiveness, and, second, on the level of the incompatibility of this divine series with God's hegemony. The Great Anonym is at odds with his abilities, which he finally manages to turn upside down, grinding them off.

It has been sometimes alleged that the world's genesis would be somehow equal to God's thinking. This theory, circulated as early as ancient times, is that of a presupposed identity between the ideative act and the accomplishing act. An idea thought by God would be *eo ipso* an accomplishment, an existential transposition. Certainly, what we have here is a mere theoretical postulate that has enjoyed the more or less overt approval of many a metaphysician. To us, the postulate is more like a pretext which allows a few quite interesting variations. The considerations that we bring in should not be rejected for the simple reason that they are based on a postulated but not demonstrated premise. These considerations have a playful and conditioned character. If we admit that the 'thought' is, on a divine level, the equivalent of an *achieving* act, we easily end up in constituting some paradoxes. Eventually, to the Great Anonym, the most natural thing would be that, through any of his ideatic acts, he should think himself, since there is nothing else besides him that can be thought. In keeping with the mentioned postulate, this would mean, though, the creation of a second God, of a third, and so on. If the process of divine creation got accomplished on the basis of the equivalence between thinking and achieving act, then, obviously, the Great Anonym would trap himself in a difficult and risky situation. It would be natural that, through any thinking act, the Great Anonym should actually think himself, but since this would breed theogony, the Great Anonym has to deny himself the pleasure of thinking the way a philosophical Narcissus would do. Under the pressure of undesirable consequences, the Great Anonym refrains himself from the global thinking of his entity, that is, from the sole thinking that would be worth the epithet of 'divine'. The Great Anonym would see himself forced almost completely to extinguish his thinking, or to think himself each time in a 'negative' sort of way, *lest he should realise himself.* In any case the Great Anonym cannot permit himself to think 'positively' except in 'differentials', namely in minimised segments. The Great Anonym's thinking, if we make abstraction of the differential or differentials towards which it is directed each time with utmost intensity, would be deliberately extinguished, or would have a negative sign as to the object. Actually, the Great Anonym thinks in a highly limited way, although perfectly adequate, whereas man thinks much more totally, but inadequately (censored). The object of divine thinking should have a maximum volume but this thinking, which involves unfathomable risks, gets stifled, restricting, for tactical reasons, its object to disparate fractions.

It would be difficult for us to decide what is, in essence, the technique of the genesis, and whether reproductionism, on which we build as if on a premise, takes place on a pure, existential and structural level, that is *ontologically*, or whether the process takes place on an *epistemological* level, basing itself on the equivalence between thinking and realisation. Since the thesis of a 'thinking' equivalent to 'achievement' is but a circumscription of magical thinking, everything makes us bend towards the former solution. In any case, if the Great Anonym followed the principle of the minimum effort, a divine series would come into being of absolutely similar existences. The effort made by the Great Anonym for the world's genesis is not an effort of creation, but an effort aimed at refraining the possible 'more'. We have to admit that nowhere in the field of existence are we given the example of such a genetic process. The world's genesis features singular, matchless aspects. Elaborating such an explanation, we have broken with any visual metaphor, while getting close to a more distilled metaphor, required by the very uniqueness of the cosmological problem.

Translated by Ileana Barbu

(B) From 'The divine differentials'

In this extract, Blaga elaborates his conception of how the Great Anonym generates the world by suppressing most possibilities of existence, and contrasts it with creation by way of a 'magic thinking' in which God's thought of something, a type or an individual, thereby brings it into existence, and with Neo-Platonic and other emanationisms. The concept of a 'divine differential', an infinitesimal and simple structure, is a 'liminal' one, which can be thought but not imagined. Here, too, Blaga rightly sees no radical difference between metaphysics and science, but one only of degree.

There is an especially particular relation between metaphysics and experience. No metaphysical outlook can hope for a *positive* confirmation at an empirical level. However, experience possesses the ability to *invalidate* a metaphysics. Any metaphysician knows that his vision cannot be converted and displayed in terms of experience. Still any responsible metaphysician uses experience as a filter. This is the reason why we are not going make one step without asking ourselves to what extent the vision we set forth is or is not contradicted by the data of experience.

Empirical things are mostly chrono-spatial individuals: that is, existences that take place here and now. Individuals are characterised by various particularities, some thoroughly unique, others featuring a diversely graduated generality. Owing to its particularities, which do not repeat themselves, the individual acquires a demonstrative, yet inexpressible, appearance; owing to its more general particularities; individuals are subordinated to certain 'types', gradually ever more abstract, and *eo ipso* susceptible of being named and determined. An oak stands in front of us: we can see it, we can touch and identify it. Owing to one of its features, the oak possesses the gift of a special presence as related to the other oaks; in front of our apperceptive act, it asserts itself as a definite individual. Its form, although resembling that of other oaks, is, due to a lot of details, *only* its own; the way its branches are set is only its own, and so are the richness and distribution of its leaves. The singular traits of the oak standing in front of us get even more singular as we plunge deeper into its very concrete matter and configuration, and in whatever we are recording through the gate of our feelings here and now. We can certainly grant a metaphysician the liberty to ask himself this question: May have God created the oak in front of me, *thinking* and *imagining it* in all these singular details, through a separate act of His consciousness? If the metaphysician's answer is affirmative, then he also has to pronounce the conclusion that God had to generate or create all the other oaks through as many separate acts, each having a singular objective. In the case of such a hypothesis, the natural event, such as, for instance, the process of fecundation, would be but an opportunity offered to God so that he may express his creative abilities. A current folk metaphysics assigns God such an excess of care for each hair on our head, and for each grain of sand. But there is also a less current metaphysics which thinks that God only created the *'type'* of the oak, be it as an ideal model, after which all real oaks are made, be it as a mysterious organising power effectively present in each oak. If one accepts such an interpretation of the divinity's creative act, then, the numberless concrete traits, conceptually inexpressible, which make of this magnificent oak standing in front of us a non-repeatable example, would be accidental and would not be part of the objective of divine acts; the singular traits may be explained rather by circumstances thoroughly detached from God's will. In the Middle Ages, a metaphysical problem of this kind had truly managed to raise a great interest and equally violent disputes. Certain Arabic interpreters of the Aristotelian philosophy would limit God's thinking to ideative acts, having as object only 'generic types'. They maintained that God thinks only in 'forms', which correspond to the general concepts, so that he, as far as the order of life is concerned (to give only an example), would be aware of 'species' only, and not of 'individuals'. Individuals as such would appear to lie outside the divinity's cognitive sphere. It is known that a few Christian scholastics accepted the challenge and entered the dispute, but only to struggle against that thesis with all the force one can imagine. The passion that the Christian put in fighting off this outlook is no wonder if we take into account the grave accent the Christian metaphysics lays on *'individual'* existence. The Arabic interpretation of the Aristotelian thinking, contesting God's ability to think and know the individual as such, could undoubtedly have shaken one of the capital pillars of the Christian doctrine. The Arabic interpretation is certainly one of the most daring theses ever advocated by the human spirit in history. As far as we are concerned, we have no intention to react against the Arabic thesis with the same feeling of panic or fear that seized the apologists of a Christianised Aristotle.

As regards the genetic technique of the Great Anonym, we have admitted the possibility of two alternative variants. Genesis can take place as a process of direct emission from the divine substance and structure, and this without the eventual 'thinking' of this process playing the role of a component of the process. But the genetic process may also take place on the basis of the 'thinking' of the object to be achieved. As I have said before, there circulates among metaphysicians the belief that God's thinking acts are *eo ipso*, acts of realising the objects thought. This thinking assimilated to the creative act is in fact a magical thinking of a maximum intensity and efficiency. According to the Book of Genesis, God said: 'Let there be light.' And there was light. In the Bible's outlook, the genetic technique would be of a magical nature *par excellence.* How should we conceive the magical thinking of the Great Anonym if the cosmic genesis had such a technique as its basis?

If, in general, we assign to the Great Anonym acts of magical thinking, then, naturally, we cannot deny his ability *magically to imagine* 'individualities', and magically *to think* the 'types' of various generality. But from among the Great Anonym's abilities, first comes one unusually natural. The Great Anonym has the capacity first to think himself magically, thus reproducing himself unlimitedly in this way. On the other hand, we know that the Great Anonym does not allow himself what he 'can', but he proceeds, for superior reasons, as a ruthless eradicator of possibilities, playing true havoc among all the possible accomplishments. The Great Anonym would not allow himself either the total thinking of his very being, nor the thinking of types or the imagining of individualities of the empirical type. If he proceeds magically, the Great Anonym will not 'think' otherwise but in 'divine differentials'. Therefore, not only the concrete individuals, but also the general types are outside the sphere of his magical thinking. For known reasons, the objects of the divinity's magic thinking must necessarily be simple and infinitesimal. These objects come into being not through the invention of a 'something' that would not exist before, but through the limitation and breaking up of an existent object, which is the very being of the Divinity. We shall not, therefore assert, like some Arabic interpreters of Aristotle, that God *cannot* imagine empirical individuals, and that he, through his nature, could only think the types. The Great Anonym can imagine individuals just as he can imagine the types, since he is best entitled to think the 'divine whole'. All these acts would, however, be *inopportune*, inopportune for the creature and inopportune first for himself, who thinks everything according to a centralist outlook. Such acts of magical thinking would lead to the genesis of identities or to the genesis of complex creatures with too great an autarchic potential, that is, to existences that would threaten the divine hegemony. Consequently the Great Anonym reduces his thinking to the objective of the differentials. And these, he does not think all, but only those which are not clearly nuclear. But once more: all these considerations aspire after a metaphysical validity only if genesis takes place on the basis of magical thinking. Actually, we tend to believe that the process of genesis takes place rather on an ontological level that is substantial and structural, than on the basis of a magical thinking, a magical thinking that we had brought into discussion more for the sake of argument.

There is no suitable term for the cosmogonic process, no term to designate this deliberately differentiated reproductionism, because this process in one of a kind. The process of genesis is not fully covered by any of these terms: birth, emission, emanation, creation, etc. For want of an authentic and circulated term likely concisely to embrace the process, we are compelled to make use of words like the ones we mentioned earlier. However, terms have only the role of guiding one's attention towards a thoroughly particular process. Thus, while using terms, like creation, birth, emanation, etc., one cannot speak about a conceptual identification of the process, but rather about a pointing gesture of human speech which has suddenly reached an uncomfortable terminological deficiency. Certainly, terms are useful to our effort, but we ought to be constantly aware of their impropriety. The prefiguration of our cosmogonic theory, as outlined above, is likely to be labelled as 'emissionistic', although the process described also catches one's attention by certain particularities that do not bring about a mere 'emission'. The act, instead of unleashing itself in complex and compact entities, limits itself to launching differentials, and not even all of the possible differentials: a *de jure* process is thus replaced by a random one. In this process, a capital role is played by the factor of a deliberate and highly motivated denaturalisation. One should point out that none of the truly emissionistic metaphysical systems has ever reached such thoughts. Emissionistic are certain Indian systems which equate the world to either a substantial emanation or to a dream of God. Equally emissionistic are so many Islamic systems, according to which the world is emitted by God, the invisible, as if he would need the cosmic colours and forms in order to make himself visible. As undoubtedly emissionistic are the Neo-Platonic Gnostic systems which see God as an endless source of similar existences, or of complex aeonic existences. Leibniz's monadical system is quasi-emissionistic, although it sometimes appears formulated in creational terms. According to Leibniz's outlook, the divine being creates *individuals* who are living images of the *whole cosmos*, a sort of Veronica's veils on which the same icon has been printed, differentiated only by clarity. Each 'monad' is a cosmic entity in miniature, a psychically introverted *world*. Any monad is endowed with a full autarchic potential, since it lives through itself, without having any connection with the other monads. We have to admit that the enumerated metaphysical systems, the same as many others, have the merit of having guessed some of the Great Anonym's possibilities, but precisely those possibilities which are deliberately avoided, that is those that never turn into reality. It is those possibilities which, being a threat to the centralism of existence, are extirpated as early as the precosmic stage! The generating acts of the Originary Source can have but one alternative objective: they generate either 'Wholes' (divine hypostatic, aeonic, typical), or differentials. *Tertium non datur*. At the right time we shall also provide certain decisive empirical evidence which show that the divine acts do not intend 'Wholes', either more ample or more limited; therefore their objective is necessarily of a differential nature. The acts generating Wholes are possible, but they remain unconsummated. The Great Anonym avoids filiation and is shy of relatives who resemble him and who, inevitably, would move eccentrically. The Great Anonym does not want to recognise himself as in a mirror in any of the results of his acts. That is why, he first mutilates them to the maximum. The well-known hero of a great dramatic poem asks himself whether in the beginning there was the Word (Idea) or the Deed. Our answer to this question is: neither one was the first. Because at the beginning there was a sort of cautious categorical and radical drawing off of the Divinity from his own generating possibilities.

Before showing the ways in which the divine differentials integrate into the stage of the indirect genesis, let us clear up a little the thought itself of these divine differentials. A divine differential is the equivalent of an infinitesimal fragment from the substantial, structural, fully autarchic, trans-spatial Whole of the Great Anonym. The divine differential is not in the least identical to the spatial, quantitative-mathematical differential. *With the divine differentials we find ourselves in a trans-mathematical region, and the mathematical differential would constitute but one case among the numberless heterogeneous divine differentials.* By means of mathematical differentials we might build a mathematical vision of space, but never cosmic realities; not even the *real* space or that X existence, that we inadequately answer with our subjective intuition about space, seem to get 'organised' exclusively on the basis of mathematical differentials, but on the basis of very heterogeneous divine differentials.

The divine differentials (we are referring now to the heterogeneous ones) are substantially as many infinitesimal bearers of a virtual structure of an extreme, ultimate simplicity. The divine differentials represent, therefore, both from a dimensional and a structural angle, something *liminal*, which makes it impossible to imagine them. But the *conceptual* thinking of the divine differentials raises a difficulty, too, even a double difficulty. The divine differentials must be considered as 'infinitesimal' (symbolically as 'points'), bearers of one absolutely simple *virtual structure*. By introducing the terms 'infinitesimal' and 'absolutely simple' in this field, we have twice to think *in a liminal way*. In order to be thought, liminal concepts involve progressively infinite psychological processes that the theoretical consciousness cannot grasp but understands 'intentionally'. Consequently, one could not assert that the difficulties faced by conceptual thinking of the 'divine differentials' would be of a nature different from the difficulty of other liminal concepts, of which not even 'science' is spared. In the case of divine differentials, these conceptual difficulties simply pile up. The concept of divine differentials imposes itself, however, for peripheral zones. The facts that for the ideation of these differentials we do not have a concrete-imaginary support, and that the very content of the concept is more intentioned and postulated than fulfilled, are not such as to forbid every intellectual operation with such a concept. Science does the same thing boldly and openly. Science also makes use of highly abstract concepts lacking a comfortable imaginary and psychological support, and even a manifest liminal seal. If science were to put us to trial for this matter, it would lose, because we would bring to our defence the solemn and irrefutable evidence of its own methods.

We have stated earlier that the divine differential would be, from a substantial angle, an infinitesimal existence. But we shall take care to add right away that the *substance* of a divine differential is not identical with any the empirical substance, or with any with which scientific theories operate. However, the *substances* of the 'differentials' *prefigure* all the others. Obviously, the divine differentials are of a 'substantial' nature, and the heterogeneous differentials also diversify themselves in respect of substance, but they will never be of a nature characterised as 'energetic' or 'material', or of a nature characterised as 'psychic' or 'spiritual'. Physical power, for instance, is a complex existence in respect of substance and structure, even under its basic form of 'quanta'. The energy quanta themselves represent, each for itself, an integration and organisation of certain divine differentials, both heterogeneous and homogeneous. Matter in its turn, even reduced to its ultimate electronic or protonic expression, is in itself an integration and organisation of divine differentials, of totally *sui generis* differentials in respect of substance. The 'psyche' and the 'spirit' are themselves the result of some processes of integration and organisation of divine differentials, of differentials again entirely unique in respect of substance. *Therefore, physical, energy has as a substratum various, yet specific, differentials, and so do matter, life, psyche and spirit: each region with its own basic heterogeneous, yet specific, differentials. Never will the divine differentials, which actively co-operate, for instance, for the building up of 'matter', be able to have as a result both 'life' and 'spirit'; to constitute these, there is need for the co-operation of differentials of a specific nature.*

The heterogeneous divine differentials diversify in point of substantial solidarity with the absolutely simple virtual structures, whose bearers they are. The source of this heterogeneity of the divine differentials is again the substantial and structural complexity of the 'Divine Whole'. *The heterogeneous divine differentials, representing in respect of their virtual structures a fragmented-infinitesimal whole, are, because of this origin of theirs, of a complementary nature. In the circumstances, we have to look for the explanation of the possibility of a process of integration within them.*

As within the sphere of the substantial and structural ensemble of the Great Anonym, we could make an opportune distinction between more central, more nuclear, more essential zones, and more peripheral or less essential zones, so the heterogeneous, divine differentials, which correspond to an equivalent number of infinitesimal fragments of the anonymous complex, will consequently accept the same distinction: because certain differentials, in respect of their source, will have a more nuclear origin, and others, a more peripheral one. Those clearly nuclear, although possible, do not come into existence, being prohibited by the system of preventing measures. This non-emission of clearly nuclear differentials actually triggers a superior line for the process of 'integration' that subsequently takes place in the universe. The processes of integration cannot pass beyond this ceiling because there are no 'divine differentials' to help them take shape.

According to our conception, the primary objective of the genetic act of the Great Anonym is still in its precosmic phase, previously degraded by the elimination of all *major* possibilities. As early as the precosmic phase, possibilities are differentiated, and, consequently, they are partially discriminated (the nuclear ones), and partially actually emitted as heterogeneous differentials. But as this preventively regulated genetic act repeats itself endlessly, we shall state that each divine differential is generated in numberless exemplars of the same sort. Each divine differential has an infinite number of copies.

With this, we have provided the outlines necessity for the purely speculative anticipation of our cosmogonic theory.

Chapter 5

From *Transcendental Censorship* (1934)

From 'Integration with Mystery'

The category of mystery, placed by Blaga in the centre of knowledge, forms the principal point of juncture between his theory of knowledge and his metaphysics: see above, the extract from 'The Divine Differentials'. Mystery represents the metaphysical nucleus of knowledge because it manifests the awareness of an essential absence. A category-idea, like soul, substance or time, mystery surpasses them as a negative idea, a unique idea by means of which Luciferian knowledge is allowed the act of transcendence. But Luciferian pride in our own abilities, which have enabled us to reach a new level of thought and understanding, may cause us to think that we can go on to abolish mystery completely and render things wholly transparent and comprehensible. Any such hopes are doomed to disappointment. We need to accept the fact of mystery, and to integrate ourselves with it. Integration with mystery is realised in three ways: by attenuating, making permanent or intensifying what is unknown. Blaga observes that previous philosophers have grasped the general presence of mystery but have tried to annihilate it by denying it. Blaga's novel concept is to accept the permanence of mystery even in the construction of metaphysical ideas **sub specie mysterii**, *in the sense in which the world's great philosophers have placed every idea* **sub specie** *certain categories.*

We already know from the study dedicated to it that Luciferian knowledge[1] starts with that act by means of which a mystery as such is considered as 'open'. On the ontological level, where all those deeds that we are concerned with are situated, the initial act of Luciferian knowledge has a peculiar meaning. From this new point of view, the initial act of Luciferian knowledge represents the act which eliminated the illusion of adequacy. By means of this act, apprehending knowledge implicitly declares itself to be *disillusioned* of its own contents. The cognitive subject behaves as if it knew that the revelations that invade individualised knowledge are only 'dissimulating revelations' of existential mysteries. Revelations are considered to be mere apparent signs of some mysteries that are, by their nature, hidden. Through its Luciferian mode of behaving individualised knowledge places itself inside the 'mystery as such'. This gift of placing itself within the 'mystery as such' is still another gift of grace: a gift that is, nevertheless, useful for the Luciferian temptation, in its restricted sense, of overflowing the pre-set 'mould'.

Let us now dwell, for a while, upon the idea of mystery, the epistemological variants of which have already been presented. We showed then, that the idea of mystery should be situated in the very core of the theory of knowledge. Let us now question ourselves whether this very idea may, by any chance, be capable of becoming the core of some ontology or metaphysics of knowledge, as well. I do think so. Here we are now at that point to which we have purposely to draw the reader's attention, requesting also some mental strain from him. Here we are now at a turn in the road or at the decisive joint point of our metaphysical theory. The vital knot of the theory resides in the assertion that the idea of mystery is located in a privileged place in the inner joint of individualised knowledge

This is because *the idea of mystery is the only one that breaks through or, better to say, 'transpasses' the front line of transcendental censorship*. We also have to add that this happens with the permission of the transcendental censorship itself. Other ideas, that may be said to be 'transpassing' the front line of censorship, only possess this quality to the extent they contain, as a last implication, the very idea of mystery as such. It may seem strange that, among such a huge number of ideas that inhabit individualised knowledge, everywhere and forever, only one *single* idea be privileged in this sense. Stripped of any additional explanations, the statement about the privileged singularity of the idea of mystery seems, nevertheless, arbitrary. It is, however, the strange Archimedean point that we cannot give up. The idea of mystery has a number of features of its own and, which, having been once evidenced, can weaken that feeling of the arbitrary conveyed by the statement about the privilege of its being the unique 'ford' that can cross the zone of transcendental censorship.

Its features may be stated as follows:

1. the idea of mystery implies a transcending act;

2. the idea of mystery is an 'idea-in-the-negative';
3. the idea of mystery forms the horizon of an entire *modus cognoscendi*;
4. the idea of mystery is a constitutive element of the definition of transcendental censorship.

By mystery, individualised knowledge ideatively reaches the transcendent object: the idea of mystery as such, with its variants, however, is only incompletely in touch with the transcendent, meaning that it portrays the *essential* part of the transcendent object only in the *negative*. We recall the definition: the idea of mystery expresses the awareness of a shortcoming in the objective of knowledge, an *essential deficiency* that can be substituted by an *accidental presence*. Individualised knowledge does have an adequate idea about the 'whole object': the idea of mystery. It consists in the awareness of an *absence* with an accent of *essentiality* that replaces a *full presence*, without, however, any accent of essentiality[2]. This makes us call the idea of mystery an idea-in-the negative. The idea of mystery covers the 'whole object', only that it does this just as the 'negative', the film or the mould covers its object in plastic techniques.

Being a transcending idea and an idea-in-the-negative, the idea of mystery keeps apart from all the others, by this very fact. Still its standing apart from all the others is caused by its expecting a role that the mind does not hesitate to accord it without any restriction. While all ideas compose a single order, the idea of mystery is of a *different order*. Whenever an idea has a certain degree of abstraction and dominance in the field of knowledge, then it is given the honorary title of 'category-idea'. Is the idea of mystery such kind of category-idea? This is the lowest degree that it can be conferred on it. However, it seems to have been born for a much higher honour. The idea of mystery means more than a category-idea, such as those of substance, causality etc. The idea of mystery circumscribes the *epistemological horizon* of an entire *modus cognoscendi*, namely the Luciferian one. The idea of mystery delimits the vast and inexhaustible object of Luciferian knowledge. Were we not to have the idea of mystery, our mind would be poorer not only by one category-idea, one among others, but by an entire *modus cognoscendi*, the most complex of those that strive for the supremacy in the human mind. The idea of mystery has a rather *continental* role on the globe of individualised knowledge.

Through transcendental censorship, individualised knowledge is compelled to act as an organ for the a*pologetic conversion of existential mysteries*. The idea of mystery is a determinant moment of this censorial ontology. The idea of mystery highlights and determines the meaning of transcendental censorship.

Its being a product of a transcending act, its being an idea in-the-negative, an horizon of an entire *modus cognoscendi* and a constitutive moment in the ontology of censorship, these are all reunited in the idea of mystery, just like many other features that vigorously plead for the assertion of its singularity. The idea of mystery is a transcending idea, so accepted by the transcendental censorship only because it is an idea-in-the-negative; the idea of mystery conditions a whole *modus cognoscendi*, only because it is the outcome of a transcending act; the idea of mystery is a constitutive moment of transcendental censorship, only because it is, at the same time, the product of a transcending act, an idea-in-the-negative and the horizon of an entire *modus cognoscendi*. The singularity of the idea of mystery and its privilege can be explained by several peculiarities that entwine with, link to, and condition one another.

Transcendental censorship, by its being true to itself, can allow individualised knowledge to break through the front line of censorship by means of the idea-in-the negative of mystery; however, it cannot allow knowledge positively to penetrate transcendence. Some form of overcoming censorship through the idea-in-the negative of mystery as such is allowed only because in this way mystery is, *de facto*, still 'protected'. Transcendental censorship intervenes with its partition zone only against any possible *positive* transcending. *It is not the transcending act in general that is forbidden to individualised knowledge, but the positive transcending one.* The transcending act via the idea in the negative is accepted since, by this act, the intentions and the purpose of censorship are not contravened. The line on which transcendental censorship has planted its interdictions does not lie between the dissimulating revelation of existence and the transcending act itself, only to accept the former and reject the latter. The line of censorial interdictions lies between the dissimulating revelation and transcending through the idea-in-the-negative, seen as a single accepted front, on the one hand, and positive transcending seen as an adverse and unaccepted front, on the other hand. Metaphysicians have not sensed the existence of a transcendental censorship, and even less have they sensed the entirely paradoxical positioning of the *censorial line*.

We are going back now. I said that through Luciferian knowledge the individualised subject follows the inner drama. Let us explain. Luciferian knowledge, having managed to enter the immediacy of the very object through the idea in the negative of the mystery, that is, to break through the front line of the transcendental censorship, falls into the sin of believing that it is able also *positively* to grasp the transcendent object. Luciferian knowledge, possessing the transcending ability (through the idea-in-the-negative), makes the mistake of thinking that it also possesses the ability of positive transcending. The going out of this state of grace at this place and time takes a turn of, and grows to proportions of, really Luciferian sizes. Ruled by the Luciferian self-conceit, individualised knowledge still strives to assimilate, to nullify mystery, by replacing it with cognitive positions that no longer imply any mystery; ruled by Luciferian self-conceit, individualised knowledge has a tendency to undo mystery by converting it into non-mystery. We are, thus, right in the core of the inner drama of individualised knowledge.

Luciferian attempts at converting a mystery into a non-mystery are tragic, since after infinite efforts they are doomed to collapse. The efforts of Luciferian knowledge themselves are hardly futile and purposeless. The tragic destiny refers more to hopes linked to such efforts, than to the efforts themselves. I repeat: Luciferian knowledge is in no way able to convert existential mystery into non-mystery. It is only able to integrate itself into mystery as such, with the liberty of 'varying' it. We also know that such integration is threefold:

1. Luciferian knowledge integrates itself with mystery making an attempt to attenuate it, without ever claiming to cancel it. This task represents an indefinite problem.
2. Luciferian knowledge merges with the mystery while maintaining it.
3. Luciferian knowledge merges with the mystery while intensifying it, to put it differently, while conferring it with all the relief and depth that it deserves.

Attenuation and perpetuation of a mystery is achieved by 'intellectual enstasy', while the intensifying of mystery is achieved by what we have called 'intellectual ecstasy'. We shall not dwell upon these terms that are deeply enough explained in my work. I should only add that intellectual ecstasy opens the possibility of extreme or total merging of individualised knowledge with 'mystery'. Since through intellectual ecstasy individualised knowledge not only gives up the ability to convert mystery into non-mystery, but it feels complaisant with the intensified mystery as such—this being a very contrary attitude—'intellectual ecstasy' gains the significance of a compensation or redemption of the initial Luciferian conceit.

Individualised knowledge, seen in its relationship with the existential mystery, is doomed, as already seen, by its very structural modes, to an inner drama. The drama we are talking about is scarcely accidental; it belongs to the inner nature of individualised knowledge that has the freedom of shifting from the paradisaic mode (either concrete or mythical), to the Luciferian one. Individualised knowledge is dramatic through its possibilities, still less dramatic through the route a particular individual takes *de facto*. The inner drama of individualised knowledge is virtual to a great extent, because in history and in isolated individuals it is achieved differently and mainly to a different degree. The inner drama of knowledge lends itself to a great degree to literary commentaries and stylistic skills. By repudiating randomly contrived artifices we limit ourselves to define the 'stages' of the drama. They are:

state of grace

coming out of grace

Luciferian conceit

failure

integration with mystery

These stages, which look as if they have been copied from some scholastic treatise on dramaturgy, are not simultaneously and equally completed in the consciousness of all individuals. It depends on the intellectual energy of each individual to what depth into this hierarchy of stages he manages to proceed with the drama virtually inscribed in the very structure of individualised knowledge. There are individuals who stick to the state of grace forever, without ever being disillusioned anywhere by anyone; others permanently keep to the Luciferian conceit, without ever sensing its futility; there are also some who keep on going until they integrate with the mystery, still without drawing any of the final conclusions out of their attitude. Few, however, are those who integrate with the mystery in the total form of ecstasy, thus completing, with an inner reconciliation, the drama of knowledge.

_*_

In the history of philosophy, the idea of 'mystery' has played a more or less deplorable role of a Cinderella. More seriously, thinkers have been frightened of mystery, just as the ancient Greeks were of chaos, just as Christians by sin. Consequently, 'mystery' has been for the various sages either a target to be immediately pushed aside or simply a presence liminal to knowledge. Whenever sages have not merely been content with sensing mystery, they have always attempted to push it aside. Such behaviour is almost equal to a phobia with respect to mystery. Whenever this is the case, we can no longer ask for advice from consecrated philosophy, as concerns the subjects approached here. The freshness of our point of view resides, as we think, in our intention of neither pushing mystery aside, nor in only acknowledging its liminal presence. We philosophise *sub specie mysterium*. 'Mystery' is for us the supreme viewpoint. Having circumscribed the variants of the idea of mystery, I realised from the very beginning that we possess a novel philosophic point of view, capable of fruition both in epistemology and in metaphysics as well. There is hardly any metaphysics without a silver peg, centrally stuck in the lawn of existence. In any metaphysics there is a word highlighted by being written in block capitals. Some have hoped for a metaphysics *sub specie aeternitas*. Here, I have to remind you of Parmenides' immovable globe and Spinoza's cosmic statics, with the rays of lights and transparencies of geometrical lenses. Others saw everything *sub specie temporis*. Let us remember the 'river' without sources and flooding, with its solemn and Acherontic murmur, from which Heraclitus sipped the poison of dejection. Some yearned for a concept of existence *sub specie materia*. This happened when 'the machine' had not yet become vulgar and was still able to enchant in the same manner as a powerful divinity would do of yore. Still others have enclosed everything *sub specie* 'of soul'. These are particularly Romantics as a rule, for whom rocks have their own life, and plants have a heart that beats seraphically with a crepuscular hymn to existence. In metaphysics, maybe more than anywhere else, the route we are going to follow depends on the depth of feeling, on the configuration of the mind, on the cravings, preferences, feet and walking-sticks of each one of us.

I think it is high time we all went on, searching for an as yet unattained standpoint for our eye.

Translated by Angela Crocus

Notes

1. We call it 'Luciferian knowledge', not because any of its acts would mean something Luciferian, namely, an attempt at overflowing one's own 'mould', but because it, through its own predispositions, is bent, to a great extent, on Luciferian conceit.

2. See the analysis of the idea of mystery in *Luciferian Knowledge.*

Chapter 6

From *Luciferian Knowledge* (1933)

From 'Minus cognition'

*Blaga believes that he has succeeded in demonstrating that the undular-corpuscular theory of light's nature is actually part of a **sui-generis** type of knowledge, that he calls 'minus-knowledge'. It is not a crisis of modern physics but a new type of knowledge that we are dealing with. We already know that Kant built a theory of knowledge that was actually meant philosophically to justify Newton's classical physics. Newton's physics only represents a particular case for modern physics. Thus, the necessity for philosophically justifying new constructions in physics means of a new theory of knowledge, is imperative. This is, essentially, what Blaga tried to achieve in **The Dogmatic Aeon** and **Luciferian Knowledge,** especially, by providing the theory of knowledge with the concept of 'direction'. Knowledge has not, as has been assumed since Kant, a unique direction (plus), to 'attenuate' mysteries, by means of a infinite theoretical process; knowledge has two opposite directions: that is, plus and minus. And there are circumstances when the 'minus' direction, is required that does not attenuate a mystery, but, on the contrary, intensifies and radicalises it, rendering it in formulas exclusively antinomic.*

Thus, the new idea appears as a 'bridge towards the cryptic' (as an apprehension of essences) in a theoretical (pragmatic) kind of thinking. The mechanistic and the relativist ideas, Blaga says, are the theoretical ideas by which Newton and Einstein, respectively, opened the horizon of a mystery, proposing theoretical constructions for the qualitative of the open mystery. Moreover the theoretical idea carries weight in the structural joints of Luciferian knowledge even when it is dismissed later on (see the idea of the phlogiston). The theoretical (paradigmatic) function can be fulfilled by a principle, a law, a category, a concept, a scheme. The achievability of a theory is one of the problems mentioned by Blaga that represents something similar to the capacity of scientific paradigms and their scope of applicability, as imagined by Kuhn. Luciferian knowledge is very often achieved through minus-cognition which means neither a lack of knowledge nor a harmless label stuck on all the mistakes of cognition, but, instead, a type of cognition conducted in a direction somehow contrary to the usual one, a cognition capable of progress and motion ahead. The minus-cognition formulas go from a minimum of incomprehensibility to a maximum of incomprehensibility, which is seen as an abstract build-up, with no correspondence in the factual world. Minus cognition is not anti-logic but metalogic; it does not deny, but, on the contrary, it delineates perceptions through new logic. It expands the unknown by defining it, by formulas. Therefore, this kind of condition is properly named minus-cognition, as against the plus-cognition which curtails the unknown.

The theoretical results of plus cognition are obtained under the auspices of the *enstatic* intellect, logic, the principle of non-contradiction. The theoretical results of minus cognition bear the mark of the ecstatic intellect, of anti-logic, of contradiction, of transfigured antinomy.

The internal structural symmetry of Luciferian cognition determines us to accept three planes of revelation of the cryptic within minus cognition, just like within positive cognition. However, the process of revelation of the cryptic of an open mystery has here a different direction, a contrary one, hence the minus sign. We shall give some examples of minus cognition from the history of metaphysics and science, as we did for positive cognition and zero-cognition, to illustrate the various types of minus cognition. This time we shall however note that the authors of the theories we shall mention have never even suspected that their theories are capable of the epistemological interpretations and results we have reached in our research. These interpretations are covered by the term *minus cognition*, which is entirely original.

1. Wundt has studied (observed in the idea of mathematical character) certain psychological phenomena, such as the sensation of musical tones, of chords, etc. It was natural for Wundt to attempt to reveal in his study the cryptic of the studied psychological phenomena. As a consequence of his research, Wundt gets to make a famous statement: 'The *whole* of the psychological phenomenon is more than *the sum* of its parts.' (For instance, the sensation of a chord is much more than the sum of the sensations of the particular tones which make up that chord.) Conceptually speaking, the statement is anti-logic. Wundt has nevertheless found phenomena capable of being described by this statement. The statement does not qualitatively alter the nature of the described phenomena, but

rather reveals them as something *conceptually incomprehensible*. The open mystery of the discussed psychological phenomena is revealed in its cryptic, and through this revelation, the open mystery is in fact enhanced. The enhancement takes place on the plane where it was opened, the α plane of the immediate interior experience.

2. Here we repeat an example we have mentioned in *The Dogmatic Aeon*. The newest branches of physics, interpreting the phenomena of light, reveal the cryptic of these phenomena through quantum theory and wave mechanics. Physics does not shrink from using theoretical concepts which are mutually exclusive but which it regards as equally justifiable. By posing the problem in question, physics does not hesitate from adopting an antinomical solution: light is regarded theoretically as being made up in its cryptic structure of *corpuscles* and *waves* at the same time. Compare the two terms and you will understand that these two terms cannot logically occupy the same place. The terms are mutually exclusive. Nevertheless, they are equally necessary in explaining light. The revelation of the cryptic is here minus. The open mystery of light is revealed in its cryptic aspect, but is thereby enhanced and not diminished. The revelation of the cryptic is done here on the β plane* (*corpuscle* and *wave* are imaginary concepts). The epiphanic aspect of the open mystery is stranded on the α plane (empirical optical phenomena).

The situation of quantum theory, wave mechanics, is one of the most emotional moments, perhaps the most emotional of modern science. The authors of the theory themselves are embarrassed. There are many people who think that the theory is provisional and that it is the expression of an obvious crisis from which an escape is necessary at any cost. The questions raised and the disquiet produced by the formulae of quantum theory cannot have a *scientific* solution. In our opinion, quantum theory in its present form is no more provisional than other theories, at it should not be at all regarded as the expression of a scientific crisis. Quantum theory and the situation it generated must be regarded from an entirely different standpoint. That standpoint can only be philosophical. In an epistemological perspective the entire situation takes on a different aspect. If we admit the diversity of directional factors in the theory of cognition and draw all the natural conclusions regarding minus cognition, then quantum theory in its present form ceases to cause unrest in itself. This quantum theory would then be part of a system of cognition as an entirely special case of the application of this mode of cognition and would be based on an epistemological state. This localisation of quantum theory would solve *philosophically* the difficulties of cognition created by the theory in question. It is strange that neither the authors of the theory nor philosophers have tried to draw the epistemological conclusions compatible with quantum theory. *Minus cognition*, of which the theory under discussion is an eloquent example, must not be regarded as a *lack* of cognition, but rather as cognition realised in a *different direction* than usual, as a mode of cognition required by the existence of mysteries of a superior order.

Here is another example: the time when physicists (and it is not long since) still held onto the theory of cosmic ether, a point was reached, because of certain optical phenomena, when the cryptic nature of ether was described antinomically. Ether was described as an *absolute, imponderable gaseous substance* and, at the same time, as an *absolutely rigid substance* (the concepts of *absolute gas* and *absolute rigidity* are mutually exclusive). Here the epiphanic aspect of the open mystery (ether) lies in the β plane and the revelation of the cryptic aspect of the open mystery (absolute gas—absolute rigidity) is also on the β plane (the minus zone).

3. Christian metaphysics conceived of the divine entity as being made up of one substance in three aspects (one being in three persons). The divine entity is epiphanic in the γ plane (that of pure understanding); this is where its mystery is opened. The cryptic is revealed on the same plane, in the minus direction, in the shape of the transfigured antinomy (on this topic see *The Dogmatic Aeon*). The thesis 'One being in three persons' is a transcendent antinomy, an unintelligible product of the ecstatic intellect. The theologies of all confessions regard the dogmas of Christian metaphysics as a *divine revelation* in a naturalistic sense or at least as an intellectual product based on *revelation*. In our analysis, where we totally ignore the truth or untruth of the statements, we regard these statements from the standpoint of their illustrative importance for the structure of cognition. In our opinion, from this standpoint the dogmas of Christian metaphysics represent extreme examples of *Luciferian cognition*, in its least usual form (that of minus cognition).

Neo-vitalist biological metaphysics mentions entelechy as the primary metaphysical factor of life. Entelechy is epiphanic in the plane, that of pure understanding. This is where its mystery is opening. According to Driesch, entelechy is *non-spatial*, but *divisible*. By division, it is not diminished by remains *whole* in each of its parts.

Obviously, the cryptic of entelechy is conceived of in the minus area of Luciferian cognition, without Driesch having clearly realised it.

I have quoted some special cases of minus cognition. The examples illustrate at least in some aspects the structural boundaries of minus cognition.

Minus cognition is generally characterised by the antinomic form of its theses. Through the operations required by a formula of minus cognition, the cryptic of an open mystery becomes even more cryptic, and the mystery is intensified, is enhanced and is radicalised. The positive use of antinomy, be it overt or covert, which is present in any formula of minus cognition, requires important supplementary explanations. An antinomic thesis can only be sustained if a synthesis is postulated. However, because within minus cognition a synthesis of antinomic terms is built such that it is neither intelligible nor capable of being grasped by intuition, it can only be justified as *the expression of an enhanced mystery*. The antinomic synthesis involved in the formulae of minus cognition is a postulated synthesis, which is beyond understanding or actualisation by intuition. Nevertheless, it remains capable of being formulated. As a conceptual expression, the antinomic synthesis reveals the cryptic of an open mystery, but because of the mode of revelation, the mystery suffers an intensification, a deepening, an enhancement, a radicalisation.

A thesis of minus cognition implying a clash of terms, an antinomy, and postulating a synthesis beyond understanding and actualisation inevitably leads to what I have elsewhere termed *the transfiguration of an antinomy*. The transfiguration of an antinomy consists of the forceful separation of terms between which there is a logical relation. A classical example of logically connected terms is offered by the metaphysical thesis of God as a single being in three persons. The otherwise unchanged, but logically connected and forcefully separated terms are *being* and *person*.

The transfigured antinomy is in fact the difference between a thesis of minus cognition and a mere dialectical thesis, which also operates with antinomies and antinomic syntheses.

Dialectic formulae are based on the immanent properties of paradisiacal cognition. The formulae of minus cognition are, however, a product of Luciferian cognition. They entail the crisis of the object and reveal the cryptic of an open mystery. However, because the revelation has in this instance the minus sign, the mystery thereby revealed is enhanced, radicalised as a mystery.

The methods of minus cognition must also be discerned from those sometimes used in time metaphysics, especially that known as *coincidentia oppositorum*. The absolute, considered beyond any category or concept, is considered by some metaphysicians a coincidence of opposites. This is merely a way of speaking quasi-metaphorically about something that is non-categorial, something forever fixed in the position of permanent mystery, on the line of zero cognition. It should be pointed out that minus cognition does not necessarily operate with non-categorial, indeterminate entities. In all cases in which it was and will be applied, minus cognition uses categories and concepts equally empirically concrete and imaginary. Up to a point, minus cognition uses categories and concepts just like plus-cognition. However, beyond that point concepts and notions it uses in connection with the theoretical revelation of an open mystery are presented antinomically, in the form of a transfigured antinomy, to be more precise. Thus, in the Christian thesis of God as one being in three persons, minus cognition uses certain categories as does positive cognition. God is implicitly characterised through categories and concepts like existence, essence, infinity, spirituality. From a certain point onwards, the attributes of God are transfigured and antinomical: 'one being-three persons.' Another example: in the case of the corpuscle-wave theory of light, the structure of light is described up to a point by unequivocal concepts like those of plus-cognition. Light has structure, spatial properties, time processes, etc. Beyond that point, however, the determinations of the structure of light (the cryptic) are antinomically displayed. Light is considered corpuscular and wave energy at the same time.

Let us underline here that minus cognition does not operate with non-categorial entities, at least not necessarily. When the open mystery that has become the objective of Luciferian cognition has an initial epiphanic aspect on one of the planes of revelation (α, β, γ) in the realm of positive cognition, the open mystery is determined through unequivocal categories and concepts. Similarly, the revelation of the cryptic of the open mystery always implies non-contradictory constructions and concepts up to a point. However, it happens that beyond that point the necessity might arise to reveal the cryptic of that open mystery in antinomical or transfigured antinomical terms. This is in fact where minus cognition begins.

Let us see what happens when minus cognition has to be used. We know what is the initial act. Somewhere on the planes of revelation of cognition, a mystery opens. For the leap into the cryptic of this mystery, an idea with theoretical function is used. Most often, the revelation of the cryptic on the basis of a theoretical idea is performed in the plus zone. Nevertheless, even if only theoretically, certain cases can exist where contradictory or intrinsically antinomical constructions are imposed based on an initial epiphanic material and a theoretical idea. Under such circumstances, understanding cognition has only three options:

1. To abandon the revelation of the cryptic based on the theoretical idea under discussion, searching for a different idea that would not lead to antinomical constructions.

2. To abstain from any theoretical construction that defines the open mystery as a *permanent* mystery. This act sometimes implies a vote of no confidence in logic, because it in fact sometimes happens that contradictory constructions are obtained through strictly logical deductions.

3. To assert strongly the theoretical antinomy as the expression of an enhanced mystery. This will be done *when the theoretical idea that leads to antinomical theoretical constructions has previously proved its high theoretical capacity, and based on it and the epiphanic material of the open mystery contradictory theoretical constructions are equally logically necessary.* (An example of this kind is the corpuscle-wave optical theory: the theoretical idea is that of mechanical mathematical determinism, which has proved its high theoretical capacity as it is the basis of the theoretical progress of exact sciences. Not accepting the theoretical idea because it would lead to antinomical constructions would mean to question all science, would lead to its failure! Quantum theory and wave mechanics face us with the dilemma of either proclaiming the failure of science or accepting formulae which have a surprising epistemological effect, which in principle imply the construction of minus cognition.)

Once established, minus cognition opens new and unusual perspectives. The invention of theories under its influence is mainly permitted each time plus-cognition fails in all its attempts to reveal the cryptic of an open mystery. Naturally, before going on to 'minus' reveal an open mystery, to radicalise it, the precaution must be taken to eliminate all possibilities of positive cognition.

To present minus cognition as a such possible mode is naturally exaggerated. This is for the very good reason that minus cognition implies the suspension of logic. Let us be clear, though. The suspension of logic through the acts of minus cognition does not mean the final annihilation of human logic. It only means the suspension of the laws of logic in some *results* of understanding cognition, and even those not at random or at anybody's whim, but based on logic itself, on the immanent methods of Luciferian cognition, and in no small measure on the epiphanic material of open mysteries. Minus cognition is an area of results, in themselves contrary to understanding and incapable of being actualised, of the understanding cognition. Enstatic intellect transcends itself and becomes ecstatic only to formulate certain results, and only when pushed by its own logical laws and the cryptic nature of the positive material to which they are applied. Ecstatic intellect cannot be a permanent state of the intellect, but a state in which it can be brought from time to time and from which it returns to its normal, enstatic state once a certain result has been established.

The theoreticians of cognition have not yet examined closely all types of metaphysical formulae in order to make the possible deductions with regard to cognition in general. In this respect there have been systematically ignored the formulae of Christian metaphysics. These formulae have been examined from various perspectives only by theologians, but even they did not realise that interesting and fruitful speculations could be made about the *interior volume* of understanding cognition. Our problem is in fact that of the interior volume of understanding cognition. This problem is not identical with that of the limits of cognition, which has been posed in various ways ever since Kant. The problem of the limits of cognition always implies the question of the validity of cognition, which is a matter of the relation of cognition and reality. The problem of the interior volume of understanding cognition ignores this relation and refers exclusively to the immanent modes of cognition, the ways in which understanding cognition is realised through its own nature. The interior volume of understanding (Luciferian) cognition is, as we have shown, much larger than philosophers are generally ready to admit. Understanding cognition includes by nature several modes of assimilating mysteries that it opens, more than philosophy dares imagine.

Minus cognition, whereby an open mystery is radicalised, is by nature capable of being applied especially to the problems of metaphysics.

In *The Dogmatic Aeon* I proposed for the first time the introduction of the factor of *direction* in the theory of cognition. The epistemological analyses in this book have confirmed my expectation that certain formulae, which by their nature infringe upon logic, are no accident, but rather a necessity to populate an area generated by the very internal symmetry of Luciferian cognition. Both in *The Dogmatic Aeon* and the present volume I have shown, with examples taken from the history of metaphysical and scientific thinking, that human spirit has been in fact exercised in the direction of minus cognition, too. The theoreticians of cognition have not reached the clear consciousness of these facts, though, and have not even guessed their importance. Of course, the incontrovertible fact that the two zones of Luciferian cognition, plus and minus, differ jarringly in terms of density—the plus zone is occupied by countless theses, formulae and theories while the minus one is virtually vacuous—should not give an unfair view on the minus zone. Reality must have the right to assert itself in philosophy. I gave an expression to this reality of minus cognition, in the hope that the near future will give it a special importance. It could be objected that I do not show where and in what way the methods of minus cognition could be applied. The limits of the approached subject forbid the application of minus cognition on a precise object. I only deal with the somewhat virtual significance of minus cognition, with its place and possible extent at the edges of cognition in general. The idea of radicalised mystery (as the special object of minus cognition) can be the focus of a conception that should be interesting in itself. Any thinker that is not a stranger to the rewarding passion for abstraction can realise this. The construction is in the destiny of philosophy, as is in that of mathematics, even if it may be gratuitous. Mathematics has built the non-Euclidian geometries. For decades these have been more or less constructions without an object. Einstein has acquired a glory similar to Newton's by pointing to the object of these geometries in the world around us. While I do not think I have philosophised without an object, I still wonder why should philosophy without an object be inadmissible? Especially when it subsequently would be proved to actually have one? It is certain that people have philosophised to an unimaginable extent, building false or inconsistent constructions based on given *objects*. I cannot see why the reverse should be avoided, perhaps from excessive caution, and I cannot imagine why constructions should not be built for their own sakes, and their respective objects should be searched for afterwards. This could be the role of others than those who indulged in pointless philosophy. Illustrious thinkers have proved through their actions the fruitful justification of this way of thinking. Their actions stand before us as an encouragement to lucid vision, and no less as a cause that could be successful time and time again.

Translated by Adrian Ivana

From Luciferian Knowledge (1933)

Editor's note:

* Blaga refers to the scheme in the preceding section, 'Permanentised mystery', reproduced here:

Fig. 1: The structure of the revelation of a mystery

	Enstatic intellect	Zero cognition	Ecstatic intellect	
Plus cognition	$+\gamma$	0γ	$-\gamma$	Minus cognition
	$+\beta$	0β	$-\beta$	
	$+\alpha$	0α	$-\alpha$	
		Origin		

This table should be read from bottom to top.

The Origin is an open mystery, that is, one recognised as a mystery, which is progressively revealed on the three levels α, β and γ, by either plus cognition or minus cognition, between which there is the mid-point of zero cognition at each stage.

Chapter 7

From *Science and Creation* (1942)

(A) From 'Two Types of Cognition'

Blaga credits animals with one type of awareness, concrete and directed towards bodily needs, but holds that man also has another one. Kant's categories function in the former, but 'abyssal' or 'stylistic' categories are necessary for the second. This second is specifically human and operates in science as well as art. This distinction, with the ramifications of the second type, some of which we shall follow in the remaining philosophical extracts, is Blaga's distinctive contribution to the theory of knowledge, and not only to that, but to the philosophy of culture, of science and art. Blaga terms them, respectively, 'paradisiac' and 'Luciferian' knowledge. By these terms he signifies that the former is serene and content with the natural truth which it attains and the ends which that truth serves; and that, in contrast, 'Luciferian' knowledge represents something of a revolt or fall, a work of pride. Corresponding to these two types of knowledge and cognition, Blaga distinguishes two types of the unknown: actual and non-actual. The actual unknown is specific to paradisiac knowledge, and is like 'puzzles' that can be resolved by the methods of what Kuhn would later call normal science. It is the unknown which presents itself as a 'hiatus unknown', a lapse, a simply empty gap in the limits of knowledge, and completes itself by enlarging experience. But in Luciferian knowledge, mystery, the 'cryptic unknown', presupposes a leap beyond a given experience with the help of a new idea, in what Kuhn would call 'revolutionary science'. The 'hiatus unknown' places itself alongside knowledge, but the 'cryptic unknown' substitutes itself, in a certain sense, for knowledge. By 'Luciferian knowledge' Blaga has begun to explain the profound discontinuity in the structure of knowledge as is now discussed in post-critical, post-analytic and post-modernist circles, and has created an instrument for the metaphysics of knowledge. In latter works, those published after his death, he softened the contrast between paradisaic and Luciferian knowledge, acknowledging the presence of elements of the latter in the former.

We have presented, in the present essay, some thoughts on the influence that stylistic categories exert upon the theoretical construct of 'science' and on the guiding of 'observation'. They enable us to take a stand on certain questions pertaining to the problematics of the theory of cognition. To this end it is, however, necessary first to recall some basic ideas of our philosophy.

On several occasions we have dwelt upon the distinction to be made between the modes of existence of the 'human being'. Man lives in two quite different horizons: in the concrete horizon of the sensible world, needed for his self-preservation; and in a second horizon, of mystery, for uncovering it. The first existential horizon characterises man as any other animal. It is not peculiar to him. It is only through the second existential horizon that man actually becomes a full human being. In other words, existence in the horizon of mystery, for uncovering this mystery, is an essential part of man's definition. That is a first framework that we must constantly keep in mind (. . .) However, the intrinsic complexity of man's being and consciousness has not yet been fully defined. If consciousness possesses a number of categorical functions organising the data supplied by the senses, we also know that the human being, while implacably established in the fundamental implicate (the horizon of mysteries) and in its corollary (the revelatory tendency), is also endowed with several particular categories (stylistic-abyssal) which guide, as it were, man's revelatory tendency and which, at the same time, help to somehow ensure the immunity of mystery. The stylistic categories enable any 'revelation' to provide some translucency towards the mysteries, but they also prevent the 'revelation' from ever becoming a positive and perfectly adequate conversion of the mystery. The stylistic categories take us beyond the sensible data but, at the same time, they prevent a perfectly adequate conversion of the mysteries. In our view, this complexity of implicates and corollaries, of functions and structures, found in the human being, is highly characteristic of this being and, at the same time, forms an indivisible whole (. . .) After all, the difficulties embarrassing the theorists of cognition arise from these theorists' excessive inclination to simplify and to reduce 'cognition' to one type. Because of these 'theories' and some other similar ones, we suggest a distinction between two types of 'cognition', irreducible to each other.

This Type 1 cognition consists in applying categories and concepts to sensible 'data'. The categories employed by this type of cognition may be regarded as inherent in the very structure of intelligence, but their number and even their kinds are not always the same everywhere. In terms of dissemination, the categories have only a rough generality, which means that some are more, and others less, general. It would appear, however, that these categories meet with no difficulty in getting generalised. Here, for this type of cognition, the Kantian categories, or others of the kind, could be, with a certain approximation, taken into account as more or less constituent factors.

To illustrate Type 2 of cognition we shall resort, by repetition, to an image that we have already employed. In this type of cognition one encounters not only the horizon of the sensible world and categories of the Kantian sort but, constitutively, also a horizon of mystery and stylistic (abyssal-unconscious) categories shaping the 'theoretical constructs' used in uncovering mysteries. The abyssal categories are in no way of a general character (as far as man is concerned), and do not even aspire to become general. They are, no doubt, a structural, if variable, inheritance of the human mind. This 'variability', itself more or less marked, does not absolve the human mind from the obligation, naturally unconscious, of serving a stylistic matrix. Never is man's mind deprived of abyssal categories, unless, perhaps, in notoriously abnormal cases.

The second type of cognition is incomparably more complex than the first and, hence, irreducible to it. In fact, the two types appear in relation to the two existential modes characteristic of the human being. The first type relates to man's existence in the sensible, concrete world, and is needed for man's self-preservation; the second type relates to man's existence in the horizon of mystery and is needed for revealing mystery. Between the two types there occurs the qualitative and complex leap of an ontological mutation. Science, with its theoretical constructs and with the results of controlled observation, takes shape in its decisive part within Type 2 cognition. Examining the structure of science, Kant, as well as the Neo-Kantian schools and every form of positivism have attempted an abusive, unacceptable simplification of science.

In general the philosophy of science, investigating both the methods and the structure of scientific constructs, seems quite willing to reduce 'science' to Type 1 cognition. This means an excessive emphasis on the sphere of sensible data as the source of knowledge— an approach imperfectly suited to the scientific spirit and orientations of today or, for that matter, of the past too. Actually, for constituted 'science', in its fullness, sensible data are only a threshold from which to attempt the leap into mystery; these data must be interpreted in the sense of certain theoretical ideal. 'Interpreting' the sensible data in the light of certain 'theoretical ideas' occurs, ultimately, in accordance with the lines of force of a 'stylistic field'. Thus science places itself, obviously, by its main intentions, by the predominant mass of its corpus of theses, in the sphere of Type 2 cognition. Biologico-pragmatic positivism, of all shades, understands the constructs of science as if they had emerged in the horizon of the given world as 'useful fictions'. This is an attempt to misinterpret the theoretical constructs of science by analogy with technology and biological organs. Since we distinguish between two mutually irreducible types of cognition, related to the two existential modes of human being, we can supply a different interpretation of the structure and role of 'science'. In our view, science reaches its supreme dignity not within Type 1 cognition but in Type 2. (. . .)

In the second type of cognition 'truth' is produced and evaluated by criteria other than in the first type. The so-called 'truth' attained to by Type 2 cognition bears the mark, or stigma, of the stylistic categories, which one never finds in Type 1. A scientist working in a given 'stylistic field' will deem, for instance, 'true' or 'verisimilar' only those theoretical constructs that follow the stylistic lines of his own 'field'. The scientist is, then, guided by a value of 'truth' and 'verisimilitude' emerging as such under the pressure of the lines traversing a stylistic field. Quite naturally, this 'value' and the constructs placed under its auspices have a high degree of instability. The 'theoretical construct' is controlled in Type 2 cognition, no doubt, by a sense of verisimilitude, but this sense is itself always guided by stylistic categories, which are historically and regionally variable.

The difference between the 'truth' value in Type 1 cognition and the 'truth' value in Type 2 cognition is of the same order as the distinction, in aesthetics, between natural beauty and artistic beauty. Just as artistic beauty cannot be reduced to 'truth 1', so 'truth 2' is irreducible to 'truth 1'. The constitution and evaluation of Type 2 truth is based essentially on criteria quite other than those in the case of 'Type 1 truth'. The two kinds of so-called 'truth', reached by cognition on the human level, are dependent on the two existential orders in which man lives: the order of the given world, on the one hand, and the order of mystery, on the other. The theoretical constructs of science and the results of controlled observations are, in terms of their intimate structure, far too complex for a simplistic, alternative characterisation by means of words like 'illusion', 'fiction' or 'adequate truth'. Certainly, the theoretical constructs of science are 'constructs' but they relate, in their intentionality, to a mystery that they mean us somehow to perceive. The fact that the 'theoretical constructs' of Type 2 cognition are stylistically structured proves that they seriously aspire to transcend the sensible data as such; that they do not manage to convert mysteries in an absolutely adequate and positive way, is due to the circumstance that the 'style' will isolate us from mystery to the extent it also brings us closer to it. This circumstance, equally tragic and consoling, is probably grounded in some ultimate secret design of existence.

Translated by Florin Ionescu

B. From 'On The Stylistic Field'

When applied to scientific creation, the stylistic matrix is defined as 'the stylistic field'. The stylistic field represents a sort of context, background or cultural paradigm which determines by means of stylistic categories the type of scientific knowledge, from observation to method and theory.

Empirical observations, maintained Blaga, obviously go hand in hand with some interpretation. Interpretations, in their turn, are marked not only by theoretical perspectives, but by psycho-social mentality, too. The numerous interpretations that accumulate in the body of science as pure and available material are far too often imbued with 'theory'; and moreover, the same material of simple observations is in reality contaminated by the 'stylistic' orientations of the human mind. 'We Europeans', notes Blaga, 'since Leonardo da Vinci, Galileo and Newton laid the foundation of sciences, since Descartes, Leibniz, and Kant legitimised the possibility of science, have lived with the belief that it is a perennial intangible and superhistorical entity. We had to experience shocks like those caused by the theory of relativity and wave mechanics to realise, in a lucid manner, that science is unstable, an instability brought about by the very historical relativity of spiritual creations of which science is a part'.

Science comprises a constructional part in which theoretical construction obviously influences by style, occur. Science, therefore, is not superhistorical: it is born in a field of socio-cultural force lines that model it. As a matter of fact, the results of science are established also on the intellectual horizon of human existence and they emerge as 'values', alike to those produced in the ethical field and aesthetic plane.

So, the stylistic field as conceived by Blaga ranks among the historical entities of the 'paradigm' type. These entities are being used today in explaining the process of scientific discoveries. This mode of interpreting the history of science enables us to understand the nature of science as closely related to the cultural context. Epistemological theories nowadays open, by necessity, onto ontology, anthropology and axiology. They have succeeded in doing it by frequently delving into the hiddenmost chambers of the history of culture.

There follows, we believe, clearly enough from the present work and from other writings of ours, that we ascribe a very deep origin to the stylistic factors. We think their place of origin to lie in the 'unconscious' layers of the mind, where they make up, as we suppose, an entire set, an active bundle of forces. The stylistic factors, which we have been dealing with, have a 'categorical' status. Hence the name we have given them: 'stylistic categories'. Some of these stylistic categories are in a kind of para-correspondence with certain categories of consciousness, with certain categories that help to organise the data supplied by the senses. 'Para-correspondence' is not exactly 'correspondence'. Para-correspondence implies that some stylistic categories are somehow reminiscent of certain categories of consciousness, although they actually represent different structures. An example: if consciousness has a categorical function, say, of 'space', which organises the immediate sensory data, we postulate that in the 'unconscious' there is another spatial categorical function, representing another structure than that of 'space' as employed by consciousness. While the categories of consciousness are meant primarily to organise the 'data' received through the senses, the stylistic categories relate to the horizon of mystery and are destined to model and guide the human mind's attempts to discover, by theoretical constructs or by controlled observation, its mysteries. The stylistic categories, having their source in the deep unconscious, and being at the same time meant to guide the mystery-revealing capacity, to lead us towards the hidden depths of existence, may also be called abyssal categories, *as if the abyss of mind had intentional references to the abyss of existence in general.* Numerically, the abyssal categories are invariably *a set*, and only together, as a 'bunch', can they form a 'stylistic matrix' capable, as such, of clarifying the stylistic phenomena. *The abyssal categories, active within a stylistic matrix, are also considered to be discrete. In other words, they are irreducible to one another and, at the same time, they are variables independent of one another.*

In the present essay we have extended the field of application of our concept of the stylistic factors to include also the sphere of creation, pertaining to *scientific* thought. In this the concept has once more asserted its power of expansion. The incursions we have made into the history of science have been as many opportunities of getting familiar with the modes of scientific thinking. This circumstance makes us hesitate for a moment and wonder if it would not be appropriate to attempt to explain our concept of the stylistic factors by resorting to a terminology that lies closer to what is usual in 'the sciences'. We here succumb to this temptation. Such a translation of our concept may actually be not a mere translation but also a source of new suggestions.

We have, then, agreed to ascribe to the abyssal categories the role of *modelling* and *guiding* 'forces'. But if all these categories are a sort of force, one could say that, owing to the factors which emit their modelling, guiding energy from the 'unconscious', the conscious mind is made to 'create' in a 'field of forces'. Let us call this symbolic-imaginary space, in which the conscious mind operates under the influence and domination of the stylistic categories, a 'stylistic field'. The term seems quite appropriate for use in this purely spiritual domain as well. In the 'physical' sphere one speaks of 'magnetic fields' traversed by lines of force, or of electric fields charged with 'tensions'. Maintaining the lucid distinction that should be made between the spiritual sphere and the physical, the 'field' image assumes suggestive and illustrative values that no one would readily dispense with. A 'stylistic field' can be imagined as traversed by very heterogeneous determining lines, as highly complex space, in keeping with our concept of the multiplicity and *irreducible* diversity of the 'abyssal categories'.

The theoretical constructs of the mind, aimed at uncovering some mystery, make up—to use the terms agreed on—a stylistic field in that they undergo modelling by the various lines of force that traverse this field. But this proposition is valid not only in relation to the theoretical constructs of the mind: it concerns also the results of controlled observation. Indeed, any 'controlled observation' that the mind undertakes with a view to discovering mysteries is also contained, invariably, within a stylistic field and is essentially guided by the lines of force to which we have compared our abyssal categories. Whenever logic and the theory of knowledge have endeavoured to look into the modes used by 'science' in its 'theoretical' and 'observational' approaches, or in its processes of ideational elaboration, it was deemed necessary to emphasise some allegedly exhaustive procedures of 'science'. Thus, stress has been laid alternately on rational deduction and its syllogistic models, on empirical induction, or on a 'miraculous' intuition which, by a special leap, can acquire ideas destined to guide the course of research. At times, counselled by common sense, logicians and theorists of knowledge have found that deduction, induction and intuition participate, with their several, equally necessary contributions, in the formation of 'science'. At one time it was noticed that science as such also has some structural articulations which cannot be regarded as arising from the aforementioned procedures. The structure of science presupposes some implicates, which are interwoven with its existence, though somehow outside the 'conscious' procedures, as it were. These are such structures as result from the previous organisation of sense-material by means of various categorical concepts. (Kant considered these structures to be necessarily related to the being of science; other theorists have accepted, at most, the transient usefulness of these 'categories'.) Having emphasised sufficiently the significance of categorical concepts and of empirical, deductive and intuitive methods for the constitution of science, it is now necessary to introduce the concept of 'stylistic field' into logic and the theory of knowledge also. This would help to show to what extent the theoretical constructs of 'science' (and the results of controlled observation) depend on the specific nature of the 'stylistic field', where scientific thought is always situated, without realising it. What effective powers the 'stylistic field' actually possesses, has been variously demonstrated in this essay. The history of science, like the history of philosophy, is full of conclusive evidence to the effect that even mere 'argumentation', which aspires to be strictly logical, will quite often appear altered, in its innermost mechanisms, by some 'stylistic field'. In fact, it is only through such 'alterations' that 'argumentation' can, always, take a *creative* turn, for if it withdrew into a strictly syllogistic approach, it would never escape from the sterile circle of tautology.

Science comprises a constructional part in which theoretical figments, obviously influenced by the categories of style, occur. Science, therefore, is not superhistorical; it is born in a field of lines of force that model it.

The values guiding man to knowledge are truth, verity; the definition of truth itself as positive adequacy of a content of knowledge to the content of the real is actually only a desideratum. What in effect man does in a stylistic field will take to be true and veridical only those theoretically a labile image of truth, because it is valid only within a certain historical and regional space, being determined by a certain cultural environment.

The process of theorising the human mind is engaged in, is not wholly inevitable, nor is it absolutely imperative in all undertakings. One has but to cast a glance at the history of science to see that it abounds in zigzags, sinuosities, failures, and in initiatives taken up over and over again. For the sake of man's self-preservation, the philosophy of science has reduced science to a type of empirical knowledge. But for science, empirical data are but a threshold; one must go beyond it and interpret them in the light of theoretical stances. Interpreting the data provided by the senses in the light of some theoretical ideas is, in the last analysis, determined by the categorical force-lines of a 'stylistic field'. Scientific fictions do not appear only on a biological-pragmatic plane as technical contrivances do; they are the outcome of a specific spiritual formality. A bunch of 'force-lines' in the stylistic field shapes the structure of ideational figments, just as force-lines in a magnetic field compel the iron filings to settle after a certain pattern.

The matrix of the Sumerian-Babylonian culture is marked by a specific spatial horizon, a multiple geminated space full of parallelisms and correspondences. It shows up in cosmology, poetry, and religion. This parallelism appears in the fiction about the two mountains, one lying at the sunrise, the other at the sunset, in the two-towered temples, in the heroes of the Gilgamesh and Engidu epics. The temporal horizon means cyclic periodicity. Mythology speaks of divine supremacies of a cyclic nature. The world is born, flourishes, decays and disappears and a new one emerges passing through the same stages. Each world has a 'cosmic' year. Cyclic periodicity is a fundamental structure of time, and it is different from another one, pendulating. Based on it, the Sumerian-Babylonians organised the empire of numbers into cyclic periods of the figures 6 and 12, producing eclipses with very big numbers and succeeding in forecasting eclipses with an amazing precision of date. The Saros cycle, worked out by the Chaldeans of Babylon in the 8th century BC, establishes the periodicity of sun and moon eclipses.

It is not by chance, that the Babylonians were the first to establish this periodical cycle of great scope for some celestial phenomena. They were seemingly predestined to this epoch-making scientific achievement because of some structural leanings peculiar to their mind. Their spirit was endowed with a category that guided 'empirical observation' exactly toward detecting cyclic phenomena. This led them also to discovering some physico-anatomical phenomena, viz., the circulation of blood, the two types of blood, diurnal and nocturnal that were correctly interpreted at a much later date.

The Indians had a particular predisposition for placing a negative element at the basis of existence. The first mathematicians to calculate with 'zero' number were Indians. Void, nothingness, the negative are somehow supreme fascinating objects for Indian thought. Exalting the negative brought them to conceiving atoms with a negative particularity—no extension, the impersonal, the abstract. They attest a kind of 'amor vacui' opposed to the 'horror vacui' of the Greeks. The zero born of the Indians would be due to a very positive attitude toward the idea of naught, of void, which was alien to the Greeks. The same spirit discovered the algebraic calculus and superarithmetics. Indian philosophical thinking takes exquisite pleasure in the most general characteristics of things, in the abstract features, beyond strictly generic forms, far and above what is pattern proper, genus and species, dwelling on the impersonal (Brahman), on the trans-individual (Atman) or on the self. Viewed in this light, it was but in the normal order of the Indian spirit to conceive the abstract, transnumerical magnitudes of algebra. The attraction felt for abstract thinking and for void is opposed to the interest shown by the Greeks for volumes and compact objects.

Islamic thinking, in its turn, tries to substitute itself for all visible forms and magnitudes, as a totally abstract existence. Substituting the abstract for the concrete, viewing the concrete only as an accidental garb of the abstract is in effect an algebrising spiritual trait. It enabled the Arabs to achieve a systematisation resembling Aristotle's biological system, this time, however, for the world of chemical elements. The spheres are the shroud of divinity. Seventy thousand veils of light separate man from God. The Arabian horizon is a curtain of waves and the great many portals of the Arab mosque (Cairo, Cordova).

If the Greeks' genuine abilities predestined them to found static mechanics, the same innate traits made the Arabs the fathers of optics; tempted by abstract and subtle, the most immaterial and sublimated of phenomena. The world's primordial, pre-astral luminosity as the first manifest sign of God, plays an overwhelming role in Islamic mythology. Another conclusive example: the spirit of Indian thought that led to the discoveries made in 1931 by Jagadis Chandra Bose. His study, *The Nervous Mechanism of Plants*, shows that plants are endowed with a connective tissue of inflow and of reactions altogether similar to a protoplasmatic excitation proper to an animal nerve. The plant propagates the excitation and one can notice an afferent and an efferent inflow, that is a reflex arc. The European science of the time wondered at the Indian researcher, because it was guided by other categorical standards than he was. What a European would deem as a great prescientific naiveté, that the plant is similar to the animal, is self-evident to Bose, who learnt the technique of scientific experiment but did not acquire a European mentality. His theoretical premises stem from the core of Indian spirituality. What governs all and everything is the category of unity, distinctions among living beings are but accessories.

*   *   *

While observing, the mind needs ideas to guide it. The observations made must be interpreted and interpreting implies anticipatory insights. There exists, therefore, as Blaga contends, controlled observation that is always underlaid by an idea. Observation is controlled by the categories of style. Seeing a trivial fact does not mean discovering it, the less so when the fact has a certain significance which asks for interpretation.

The light in which the Arabs study the chemical processes, for instance, is based on the idea of the changeability of elements. So, alchemy emerged, trying to control, by magic, the transformation to noble metal. The same idea led to searching for the philosophers' stone. 'The philosophers' stone' is the false problem of Arab science, just as the quadrature of the circle is the false problem of European mechanics. The philosophers' stone is the illusory problem of an excessively scientific mind, keen on the changeability of matter. The quadrature of the circle is the illusory problem of an excessively scientific spirit concerned with the dynamic, mechanical aspect of nature. The Indians are dominated by the infinite horizon, the Greeks by the finite (spherical) horizon. Therefore, they admit of the idea of plurality of spheres (Ptolemy). The Greeks have a limited horizon: the typical ideal forms materialise in the idea of the sphere, with the idea of the infinite ranking second.

If these ideas could make sense when referred to the beginnings of science, involving the stylistic field in the present scientific creation is hazardous. Nevertheless, it is worth thinking that a number of achievements might be viewed in a syncretic light, for instance: biological preformation and the monadism of Leibniz; the extraordinary imagination that led Robert Mayer to advance the principle of conservation of energy, with Cuvier's catastrophe theory, with Delacroix's art and the philosophy of Fichte; or physics and Mach's philosophy of sensation, with Manet's impressionist style, with Bergson's passion for nuances and intuition; or Einstein's conceptions of relativistic physics with expressionism in painting and the work of Brâncuși, with the art of Barlach and Arhipenko in sculpture. All these facts of culture are stamped by the same horizons, attitudes and formative openings characteristic of stylistic fields from which are detached typical representatives in science, philosophy and art. If we recall the interesting results yielded by archaeology concerning the value of the archetype in culture, the connection established between the imaginary and temporality, between mathematics, music and architecture as having the same structure of successive patterns, together with the many epistemological and historical entities through which scientists today are trying to explain the evolution of science against a cultural background. The spiritual substance craving for a temporal framework affords three possible horizons: fountain-time open to the future, cascade-time open to the past, and stream-time, a ceaseless flow of equal moments.

In the history of human thought, often more dramatic than the history of facts, metaphysical conceptions of existence have always assumed a certain temporal horizon. Fountain-time appears in Hebrew culture, in the cultures and religions that look into the future from a messianic, ascendant perspective. It is found with Hegel who conceives time as a staircase on which the idea mounts; it occurs in historical contrivances, in the evolutionist theory where transition from chaos to cosmos, from lower to higher equilibrium follows a temporal evolution. The past and the present are steps leading to the future. Time implies value-generating increases, underlying all progressive ideas.

* * *

The cascade-time is specific to the Hellenic culture (Gnostic and Neo-Platonic systems). It admits of the existence of a supreme substance degraded by time. Both the cosmic powers and mankind experience an involution as time passes by. All that has temporal priority has value priority as well. This is the time of the old mythologies, the Babylonian myth of the genesis, Platonic metaphysics, Hellenic philosophers; time is space with them all, a divine supracosmic focus, whence the logos emerges, creating the sphere of ideas, and subsequently the sublunar world: the earth, man, matter. This is a depressing vision, Blaga writes, and to annihilate the disastrous effects of the cascade-time, man is going to believe in miracles.

The stream-time is a homogeneous environment that records permanent transition. The static conceptions about the universe conceive history as a succession of interconnecting phases. This is the outlook professed by Rickert and Windelband, with the world seemingly made up of moments, facts, and monadic epochs, each being circumscribed to its own value, to its own bounds.

The theory of categorical doublets affirms that there exists in the mind, at the level of the conscious and of the unconscious, a behavioural, formative space-and-time perspective. The sensitive horizon does not express the true nature of the conscience, it is simply the inherent framework of its objects. Well now, the spatiotemporal horizon is structurally attached to this framework. Any of its changes reshuffles the intellectual framework. There is an organic solidarity between the spatiotemporal horizon and man's creations, science included. Being an indeterminate framework, the space-and-time dimension of the conscious remains the same, while the space-and-time horizon of the unconscious, being a determined framework, can no longer be one and the same for any subject, irrespective way to the realm of the conscious through scientific, artistic and metaphysical creation.

Translated by Florin Ionescu

Chapter 8

From *The Genesis of Metaphor and the Meaning of Culture* (1937)

(A) From 'The Genesis of Metaphor'

In the following extracts, Blaga develops his theory of the 'ontological mutation', produced by cultural creations in the process of the birth of revelatory (distinct from 'manufactory' or 'plasticising' ones). It is by means of revelatory metaphors that we try to apprehend and convey a mystery, that is, something quite new and beyond our existing terms and concepts and for which we have to create a new language. The stylistic elements that we are going to study among several peoples, explains Blaga, from archaic times down to the present, are not meant to be summary expressions of some hazy psychological inclination, but true modelling functions, of 'categorical' status, pertaining to the unconscious mind. Our interests do not concern matters pertaining to national psychologies, but to a possible doctrine of 'spirit', which we endow with heterogeneous sets of categorical functions. Such a doctrine, once fully clarified as to its intentions, could possibly be known as 'abyssal noology' (noos = mind, abyssal = unconscious).

The 'style' of a work of art or of a cultural creation evinces many aspects of which some at least have a certain depth and a 'categorical' sense. The latter have the character of an horizon, of an axiological atmosphere, of orientation, of form. We have dealt with this side of the creation of art or culture in *Horizon and Style*. What else we have to say along the same line of thought will come later, the more so as many surprises still lie in store for us; some of these are very important for philosophy in general and others have a deep-going metaphysical significance. Yet, before we dispel the mists which are the abode of such surprises let us extend our remarks upon another aspect of creation. Obviously, stylistic elements do not exhaust creation. A work of art and a creation of culture in general possesses 'substance' as well as style. For the moment, we shall have to leave out the kind of style which is clothed by the substance and ask ourselves which are the characteristics of the substance itself, in its most general aspects. The substance of a work of art, of a cultural creation, includes everything that is matter, sensuous element or content, an anecdote or an idea, no matter whether it is concrete or abstract, tangible or sublimated. Let us anticipate: unlike the substance of real things in the universe of the senses, the substance of something created has no signification and no meaning in itself; here substance always stands for something else; here substance is a precipitate which implies a transfer and a yoking of terms belonging to different spheres or domains. In this way the substance acquires a 'metaphorical' aspect.

This remark may cause many eyebrows to rise. The reader will probably shrug and ask: 'All right, but isn't metaphor part of the style itself? Isn't the chapter on metaphor one of the most important in all textbooks of "stylistics" that have ever come out of the printing presses everywhere in the world?' The question is psychologically justified, but its being raised is due only to a widespread preconception. In what follows we shall try to defend the other way of looking at things.

Before extending the significance of 'the metaphoric', let us analyse metaphors in the usual sense of the word. We shall limit ourselves to linguistic metaphor. There are two types or two large groups of such metaphors:

1. Manufactory metaphors
2. Revelatory metaphors

Manufactory metaphors are produced by putting together two more or less similar facts, both belonging to the given, imagined, experienced or apprehended world. (. . .)

. . . . As we said at the beginning, there is yet another type of metaphor, 'revelatory metaphor'. While the first type of metaphor does not increase the signification of the objects it refers to, but only reshapes their direct expression, the word as such, the second type of metaphor increases the signification of the very objects they refer to. Revelatory metaphors bring to light something hidden, something concerning the very facts they concentrate upon. Revelatory metaphors try, in fact, to reveal a 'mystery' by the means put at our disposal by the concrete world, by the experience of the senses and by the imaginary world. (. . .)

Revelatory metaphors result from the specifically human mode of existing, from existence within the horizon of mystery and revelation. Revelatory metaphors are the first symptoms of this specific mode of existence. We do not idealise the situation when we say that revelatory metaphors also testify to the existence of an anthropological level, a deep level given to man together with his being. As long as man (not yet a full 'Man') lives outside mystery without being aware of it, in an undisturbed state of paradisaic-animal harmony with himself and the world, he uses manufactory metaphors as the only ones required to solve the discrepancy between the concrete and the abstract. Revelatory metaphors are used when man becomes 'Man' indeed, that is the moment he places himself within the horizon and the scope of mystery.(...)

Translated by Anda Țeodorescu

(B) From 'The Uniqueness of Man'

On the one hand, man does not have absolute knowledge, but, on the other, he has risen above the level of animals. It is this second differentiation of man that Blaga now explores. Animals can use, as well as man, intellectual categories which help them to orientate themselves, giving them concrete awareness and collective security. But with man was produced an 'ontological mutation' by the birth of a new mode of existence, that in culture. Biological evolution terminates in man, who has the 'qualitative uniqueness' of existing in mystery and to reveal, by categories of the unconscious, that which radically differentiates him from the animals. Those categories will be discussed in the extracts which follow this.

Let us now see what perspectives are offered by the philosophy presented in our lectures. Undoubtedly, the animal, as an individual in which a sort of consciousness flickers, exists visibly bound to 'the immediate'. The animal consciousness does not leave the realm and the shapes of the concrete. In animal behaviour everything that seems to go beyond the immediate is due to the purposive workings of life as such and is integrated in a sort of anonymous stream gushing forth into the 'species'. We can therefore safely assume that the world of the animal-individual (the latter understood as a nucleus of consciousness), is organised like man's world, within some functional frameworks (in conformity with certain *a priori* conditions) which may vary from one species to another. Seen in this light, human intelligence is probably characterised only by a more marked complexity; the difference is therefore one of *degree*. On the other hand, the animal is completely alien to 'existence in mystery and for revelation' and to the dimension and complications which result from this mode of existence. Existence within mystery and revelation is an exclusively human mode. Specifically human is, accordingly, the whole train of consequences which derive from this mode, namely man's creative destiny, its impulses, mechanisms and limitations. An animal may produce tools, shelters, organised structures; its acts do not stem from the conscious existence through mystery and revelation; its acts are not 'creative'; they are stereotypes born out of its concern for security for itself and especially for its species. Existence within the immediate and for safety is of course a mode which the consciousness of no animal can surpass and in this category we include both inferior animals as well as those much praised for the superiority of their intelligence or instincts. Yet, man is entirely different! Man is entrapped by his creative destiny in a marvelous way; for this destiny man is capable of casting off—even at the risk of self-destruction—the advantages of equilibrium and the joys of safety. What an animal may happen to produce—hiding places or organisational structures, for instance—may be exclusively understood as a result of its vital needs. Its productions correct or compensate the vicissitudes of the environment and ensure the animal's existence in an environment, otherwise unsatisfactory from many points of view; the respective productions have no revelatory-metaphorical character nor any stylistic aspects; they are not genuine 'creations'; they never form a world apart and do not require to be judged according to norms immanent in themselves as is the case of all man's cultural creations. Cultural creations can be and are judged according to immanent norms, according to rules whose bases are in a sense interwoven with man's creative destiny and geared to it. Saying this, we do not refer to man's *abyssal categories*, namely those profound categories of the unconscious which constitute the 'stylistic matrix'. If we agree that the animal is endowed with immediate cognition, we can safely assume that it has certain functions needed for organising its world, that is, a type of 'intellectual categories'. Yet, by all tokens we can *not* ascribe *abyssal categories* to animals. The psychic structure of the animal, cognitive and fabricating, is not made up of doubled, tiered sets of categories, but, at best, of a single range, especially of the categories of concrete cognition. The animal may produce shapes and implements but these shapes have not been generated by a matrix of abyssal categories but by some vital need and are built through repetition, stereotypically, by instinct; they are always the same. The animal does not produce in order to reveal a mystery, but purely and simply in order to secure its own existence and that of the species. One can assert that the animal, as a species, may, in a sense, be the *author* of a 'civilisation'. The students of the complicated ways and habits of the ants and bees give us surprising details which are indeed amazing. Still, this animal civilisation is in many ways different from human civilisation. The state organisation of ants or bees is marvelous, indeed, but at a closer look one notices that its bases are far less complex than the analogous human structures. With the ants and the bees it is only a question of a prudential existence through the immediate, of an emanation of vital needs and of concern for the safety of the group. In the human order, state organisation and its structures somehow go beyond this goal, and, at least indirectly, bear the stamp of man's creative destiny beyond man's pure instinct of self-preservation and criteria for safety. The human state, the same as all products of civilisation, bears the stamp of abyssal categories, a stylistic stigma. That is why the forms of man's state organisation are so varied and change so often in history. They indirectly reflect 'the stylistic matrix' of the human group to which they belong. Animal civilisation, unlike the human one, is 'non-stylistic' and 'non-temporal', that is, non-historical and non-creative. Unlike the animal, man does not exist only through the immediate and for safety but at another level as well; he lives through mystery and revelation. It is therefore man alone that has a creative destiny which modifies and even changes biological laws. The significance and the implications of this destiny on an ontological, psychological and metaphysical plane have been discussed in other chapters which would enable us to dispense with repetitions. Yet, let it be said once again: before he could become 'Man', man suffered not only a *mutation of biological structures* but also an *ontological mutation.* In an *inexplicable* biological outburst, a *new* mode of existence, *unique* in the universe, declared itself in man: existence within the scope of mystery and for revelation. This mode makes man totally different from the rest of the animal world. From the metaphysical point of view, one more thing ought to be added: man 'creates' in order to reveal a mystery: his creative act goes beyond the immediate but is limited by 'transcendental brakes'. These are metaphysical aspects which can in no way be attributed to the animal, who, at best produces in order to correct or compensate the imperfections of the environment to the extent required by the need for self-preservation.

The animal is fully characterised by the following features:

1. It exists exclusively through the immediate and for safety
2. It knows the concrete world in its own way
3. The animal can be attributed certain cognitive categories in a functional sense.
4. The animal can produce civilisation but it is a non-stylistic stereotype, a non-temporal one.

Unlike the animal, man is characterised by the following features:

1. Man does not exclusively exist through the immediate and for safety, but within the scope of the mystery and for revelation too
2. Man is endowed with a culture-creating destiny (culture is metaphorical and stylistic)
3. Man is endowed not only with cognitive categories as is the animal, but with abyssal categories as well.
4. Man has the possibility not only of 'manufacturing', but also of 'creating' a civilisation, variable in stylistic and historical terms.

Let us admit that the species of beings on the earth appeared indeed as a result of evolution and *especially by biological mutation*. Making a concession to the mythical approach, the result can also be formulated as follows: both animals and man are, as 'species', *object*s of a creative act (biological mutations) but it is man alone who is also a *creative subject* (as a result of ontological mutations). With man something completely new appeared in nature. With man 'the creative subject' in the full meaning of the term appeared in the universe. This could mean that man stops being an object or material for a new biological creation. The fact that man has become Man, that is creative subject, thanks to a decisive ontological mutation, could, of course, signify that man *completed* evolution which works through biological mutation; it could therefore mean that no superior biological species is possible beyond him. This proposition could be also formulated as a question which deserves not only to be asked, but also to be thoroughly considered. In any case, Nietzsche's biological conception about the superman as a possibility for evolution in the future, was too hastily constructed without taking into account man's *qualitative singularity* and his exceptional position in nature. If man were simply an object, a bridge or a material for new biological creation (man-superman), we do not see why man should manifest himself so fully and vigorously as a subject with a creative destiny, taking upon himself great and tragic risks and renouncing even his natural equilibrium and safety. The fact that man is such a subject seems to be rather an argument that biological evolution was *completed* in man. No new and higher biological type can come out of man. Man is an end: in him the potentialities of biological mutations have been extinguished because they were completely realised and because he suffered a decisive *ontological mutation* which left behind all the other species.

Translated by Anda Ţeodorescu

Chapter 9

From *Horizon and Style* (1935)

(A) From 'The Phenomenon of Style and Methodology'

'Style' is one of Blaga's fundamental categories. Precisely because man exists in a cultural world, style pervades all his works. It denotes the specific way in which a person, group, nation or civilisation perceives, comprehends, copes with, lives in, and makes things in the world. In this excerpt from **Horizon and Style** *Blaga demonstrates that there exists a certain stylistic unity manifested in the structure of a work, the work of a person, and that of a culture as well as of a spiritual epoch. There is never an absence of style and what appears to be such is really a chaotic mixture of styles. The highlighting of a stylistic unity presupposes, besides distancing, an effort at rapport with the details of the whole and with each other, and especially a rise to a synthetic view.*

Blaga points to the fact that one of the more complex and difficult problems of knowledge is the definition of the phenomenon of style as it exists ontologically, that is, it represents much more than is specified by 'the will to style' referred to by his predecessors. A work of art, a social institution, a moral precept, a mathematical idea, are facts which, in the full sense of the word, are moments in the order of a conscious intentionality as conceived by the phenomenologists and the morphologists of culture. To this Blaga adds an absolutely original element, an existential, 'abyssal', stylistic determination of the of human manifestations. He founded 'abyssal noology' as the discipline interested in the structures of 'the unconscious mind.

However disparate the questions discussed in this book might seem, they all merge into a single one. We intend to speak about 'stylistic unity' and about the hidden factors conditioning this phenomenon. We think that the area we chose to investigate ranks, if not with the most arid ones of all philosophy, at least with the most complex and the most abstract at the same time. Naturally the subject has also less forbidding aspects or even friendly and attractive ones, which are suitable for the subtlest comments and analyses, and especially for a prodigious and exciting flight of fancy. As far as we are concerned however, what attracts us to this problem does not lie in its complications and possible superficial adventures, but in a more serious and difficult side which it possesses. The 'stylistic unity'—of a work of art, of all the works of a personality, of a period in its entire creative production, or of a whole culture—is one of the most impressive phenomena susceptible of philosophical interpretation. Style, an attribute in which the spiritual substance flourishes, is the imponderable factor through which lively unity is achieved in a complex variety of meanings and forms. Style, a bundle of half-hidden and half-revealed marks and motifs, is the coefficient through which a product of the human mind acquires the supreme dignity it can aspire to. A product of the human mind becomes sufficient unto itself primarily through 'style'. Setting out to explore several planes concurrently, we declare from the very beginning that we have decided on a cornerstone: style is a dominant phenomenon of human culture and somehow it belongs to its definition itself. 'Style' is the permanent medium in which we breathe even when we do not realise it. Indeed, sometimes people speak of 'the absence of style' from a work or a culture. If this phrase is considered more carefully, it proves to be inadequate. It defines a situation, but it worsens it unreasonably. We have enough reasons to suppose that man can only create within the framework of a style. Indeed, everyone who is conversant with the history of culture, the history of fine arts and ethnography, acquires the firm impression that there is no stylistic vacuum in the creations of imaginative thought. What seems to be an absence of style is not an 'absence' proper, but rather a chaotic mixture of styles, a superposition, an interference. A situation characterised as 'chaotic mixture' is rather precarious, but it does not contradict our tenet about the impossibility of a stylistic vacuum.

Generally speaking, it took man a long time to realise that he lived permanently in the framework of a style. This late awareness is accounted for by the fact that the presence of style, and particularly of its deepest layers, is fairly even and unbroken in a certain place and for a certain time. Style is a supreme yoke under which we live but which we only seldom perceive as such. Who feels the weight of air or the movement of the earth? The most overwhelming phenomena evade us; we cannot sense them because we are involved in them. This applies to style as well. My use of such grand terms of comparison should surprise nobody. We will quickly be persuaded as we advance in our research that style is indeed a force which we cannot control, and which keeps us bound, permeates and overpowers us.

As a rule we first notice style in others, just as we first sense astronomic movement in the coordinates of other stars and planets, not in our own planet, in whose space and movements we are caught. To discover a stylistic unity, to highlight it, one has to leave that unity, that is, to consider it from a distance. Considering a phenomenon from a distance is a primordial condition for obtaining the system of reference points required in order to describe and classify the phenomenon.

The concept of style has spheres of various sizes. We move in a smaller sphere when we speak about the style of a picture, and in a larger one when we speak about the style of a period or of a whole culture. In all these applications, the concept of style actually remains approximately the same; it only becomes more abstract or more concrete and the number of concrete items it subsumes grows or declines. The larger the sphere of a style, the more difficult it is to establish its hegemonic presence. Besides consideration from a certain distance, drawing out a stylistic unity implies an effort to relate details to the whole, details among them, and, last but not least, ascent to an overall view. If there is no permanent contact with the details and no steady ascent to the ruling unity, the concept of style remains inaccessible. A unilateral crippling of our faculties of transfer to the concrete or of shift to the abstract deprives us of any possibility of access to the phenomenon of 'style.' It is still a plausible hypothesis that sensitivity to style, the special gift which enables us to understand styles, is also the result of the analytical and synthetic qualities of the mind, not only of the senses. It is the sensitivity to style required to identify a style, not that which might underlie the creation of a style. The formation of a style, a phenomenon composed on the bass staves, is mostly due to unconscious factors, whereas the identification of a style is a matter of consciousness. The production of a style is a primary fact, similar to the facts in the six days of the Book of Genesis; the identification of a style is a posterior fact, a Sunday retrospect. The production of a style is an abyssal fact of crepuscular proportions; the identification of a style is a secondary fact, determined by the interests of a watchful subject who simply wants to know. But 'style' is one of the most complex and most difficult problems facing knowledge.

The richer and more widespread the sphere of creations considered in terms of style, the more categorical the intervention of the power of abstraction required to establish a style, and the more flexible the power of vision. It is not a very difficult thing to embrace the few characteristic notes of Rembrandt's style; but it is incomparably more difficult to render evident, for example, the unity of style under which the *disjecta membra* of the Baroque gather to recompose a huge but secret organism. The difficulties increase when, besides works of art, we also take into account the productions of metaphysical thought, or even institutions and social structures. One must have acquired some knowledge of flight and of gliding over details if one wants to embrace the French classical tragedy, the metaphysics of Leibniz, infinitesimal mathematics, and the absolutist state, and to include them in the same stylistic whole. It is only from a great commanding height that one will be able to detect the common stylistic traits of these different historical moments the contents of which are apparently wholly disparate. (Such common traits are: the thirst for perspective, frenzied passion for wholeness, the spirit of hierarchical order, excessive trust in reason, etc. It is from such traits that we recompose 'the Baroque'.)

The phenomenon of 'stylistic unity' is not a conscious invention, an aim which the mind deliberately pursues; in fact, lucid mental engineering is much less productive than people believed it to be. A conscious plan can never fully replace the axes of organic growth.

The phenomenon of style, a transplant of sap that is as heavy as blood, is deeply rooted in nests which are beyond the reach of light. It is true that style comes into being in connection with conscious human concerns but the forms it takes hardly depend on the order of conscious determinations. A borderline tree, style has its roots in another land, whence it draws its sap, unchecked and duty-free. Style comes into being without our wanting it and without our knowledge; it partly enters into the cone of light of consciousness like a message from the realm of superlight, or like a magical figure from the great dark tale of earthly life. The question: 'What are the substrata of a style?' takes us to the dangerous and delightful thresholds of 'birth-giving nature'. In fact, nothing is easier than to demonstrate how little consciousness is involved in begetting the phenomenon of 'style'. Even if creators learn that they are the parents of spiritual facts, they only dimly, or barely, realise the deeper stylistic character of their products. In most instances creators are not aware that their work implies emphases and attitudes, and also bears a formal mark which they did not intend to put in it. From this point of view paternity becomes problematical. It is true that the authors of spiritual works do not fully ignore the stylistic forms and articulations of their own works; they are surely aware of certain stylistic aspects of their works, but these are external aspects. And style does not consist only of visible petals; it also possesses several rows of covered sepals and a somewhat subterranean and fully hidden stem of forms. When aestheticians first discovered that style was a unitary patrimony of forms, emphases and motifs of a region or period, they were so surprised to find how these had an inner logic and consistency that they believed the phenomenon should be attributed to a specific 'will to form'. An amazed and helpless error of interpretation thus became established in aesthetics. It was an interpretation which could be satisfactory for a moment, but not forever. In the meantime, we have grown fairly accustomed to the natural, fully unintentional, grandeur of the phenomenon. The result is a new attitude due to which we are inclined to regard style as a phenomenon which, as far as its essential core is concerned, occurs in the absence of, and sometimes in spite of, any intention of consciousness, not as a result of a consciously maintained 'will to form', which is a figment. As a rule, only those people who geographically or chronologically live and breathe in the spirit of another stylistic unity are in a position to become aware of the 'stylistic unity' of the works belonging to a certain region or time. The simple fact of being integrated in a style prevents awareness of that style. In the period of their purest style, the ancient Greeks most probably did not even suspect the correspondence of style which nowadays we establish without any effort between a temple on the Acropolis and Euclidean mathematics, or between the sculpture of Praxiteles and the metaphysics of Plato. It is also highly probable that the nameless authors of the Gothic cathedrals did not even dream of a connection between the form of those buildings and the abstract architecture of scholastic metaphysics, which bore the mark of one and the same style, and that these different products of the human genius possessed a common stock of forms somewhere, in their foundations. Creators are always much more rooted in their style than they can possibly know. Creators usually have only a peripheral awareness of their style. The Italians must have been the first to grasp the notion of Gothic style; those Italians who had an old culture, who persisted in the Romanesque tradition and refused, with all their being, to see in the Gothic phenomenon anything but a serious drawback and a risk of barbarisation. The idea these Italians formed of the Gothic style was tantamount to a reaction; they perceived the Gothic style as a bundle of negation, a forest of lines of darkness as yet untamed, a deeply reprehensible departure from an eternal norm. Nevertheless, this reaction implied apperception of a unitary phenomenon in a mass of chaotic appearances. A huge stride had to be taken from such a reaction, which had a wide apperceptive scope but was negative, to the positive view of the Gothic style. Let us note that the decisive step was taken unhesitatingly as late as Romanticism. Opposing the classicist tradition on many points, the Romantics, urged by a secret affinity, were the first who considered the Gothic phenomenon with eyes wide open; they appreciated it as such, with all its aspects, and even exalted it. One can clearly see from this one, historically verifiable, example what a distance separates the 'knowledge' of a style from the 'phenomenon' itself.

In general, the concept of style is a comparatively late gain of the European mind. Such a concept could not have emerged as long as a community that was creating a style lived confined in itself. And until about one hundred years ago, Europeans lived, successively or alternatively, in such isolating circumstances. The more abstract concept of style could only take form when people got unexpectedly into contact, in succession or all at once, with several styles that were alien to them either because they went to other regions or because of the revival of the historical spirit. Concurrently with the flourishing of historical studies and with a growing flexibility of European sensitivity to style, the very idea of style developed, gradually gaining in scope and depth. We need not recall that in the beginning people spoke of 'style' only in connection with works of art. Once formed, the concept of style proved to bear fruit; also focusing a beneficial theoretical interest, it was then gradually refined and greatly expanded. It included a growing range of products of human activity. The concept of artistic style gradually led to that of 'cultural style'. In its broad sense, the latter is quite recent. It crystallised at a time of acute conscious criticism, in an historical phase of intellectual saturation, when the European mind permeated by the taste of decay, delighted in a highly anarchical mixture of styles. Emerging in a period without distinctive features and with a low stylistic level, the notion of 'style', in its latter meaning, was coupled with exciting reformist concerns. With Nietzsche it was accompanied by regret and had a dreamlike halo: style was the apanage of a romantic past and a motive for prophetic attitudes, pathetically maintained. In the light of this notion of style, Nietzsche condemned in particular a colourless and faceless present. Later on, when the concept rid itself of Romanticism, it was consolidated and developed as lucid, wide and pure philosophic meditation. With Simmel, Riegl, Worringer, Frobenius, Dvorak, Spengler, Keyserling and others, the concept of style becomes almost a purely cognitive, dominant 'category' through whose frame all creations of the human mind are viewed, from a statue to a conception of the world, from a canvas to an institution as important as the state, from a temple to the intrinsic idea of a whole human ethics. At moment, the concept of style practically won a categorical position. We are so used to blaming the present that nothing in it finds favour with us. Yet our time deserves some praise. We live in a period of generous understanding for all times and places and of a highly flexible sensitivity to style. This is an aspect which we should take into account if we wish to relieve the complex of inferiority which holds us in its grip. In no other period could Europeans pride themselves on such a capacity of sympathy and understanding for spiritual products from other times and other places. In no other period did sensitivity manifest such universal responsiveness. This power of conscious understanding has even attained the impressive proportions of a record and we do not know how it could ever be topped. Can anybody tell us when and where realities so alien to our continent as the African spirit, or the ancient and mediaeval American spirit, or the Asian spirit were the object of such a comprehensive sympathy as they are today on this late European soil? Obviously, we shall not overlook the reverse side. Indeed, concurrently with the immeasurable growth of understanding for styles everywhere and from all times, 'stylistic unity' in its primary meaning of a massive phenomenon seems to have vanished, making room for mixing and promiscuity. Are 'style' as a massive real occurrence and 'flexible sensitivity to style' alternative phenomena which jealously contend for complete possession of the human soul? In a sense style, as a general phenomenon, and keen consciousness of style may be swords that do not go into the same sheath. Naturally this is only a general opinion on a probable relationship of exclusion. However, the relationship of exclusion in neither necessary, nor unavoidable. Exceptions are possible and they do not impair the natural order of things. History offers us many examples that have the gift of mitigating the pessimism which assigns to consciousness an exceedingly sterilising function. Leonardo, who was unquestionably the most creative genius of all times as well as one of the most conscious and keen spirits of mankind, is an eternal and decisive proof that 'style' and 'consciousness' can also complement each other with incontestable advantages for both. Creative power and deliberate engineering have combined in a precious alloy more than once and these are rare and truly superior episodes in the history of mankind. The fact is fully verifiable. The works of Leonardo-like creators, of Edgar Alan Poe, of a playwright like Hebbel,* of Paul Valéry, silence even the most clamorous arguments to the contrary.

The history of the arts and the morphology of culture have won considerable merits in the past few decades through a splendid effort of research which has thrown light on the phenomenon of 'stylistic unity'. Researchers in this field have mainly endeavoured to highlight the phenomenon itself, by bringing it into bold relief. Prior to being explained, the phenomenon had to be identified as such. However, in this case even more than in the case of other phenomena, 'identification' raised discouraging difficulties. Thanks to the efforts they made, the phenomenon now seems more natural to us than it could look to those who noticed it first. But this perspective is very recent. Let us recall that for hundreds upon hundreds of years people were blind to this ubiquitous phenomenon. The first who succeeded in cutting the relief of unities of style in the apparently anarchical variety of human creations must have felt immense satisfaction. Their discovery almost amounted to creating something out of nothing. Their satisfaction must have been as keen as that which Goethe felt when he heard of the feat of an English naturalist to whom it had occurred to classify the clouds by 'types'. We must admit that it was not a trifle to put together the disparate and whimsical appearances of cultural creations into consistent and substantial blocks. To regard the various periods or cultures as unities of style indeed means to put order into the realm of clouds. It is an impressive idea. The work of putting into order, carried out under this sign for several decades, is fully entitled to claim this title and epithet.

Let us proceed to a more arid question. Style as a phenomenon poses some delicate problems to philosophical methodology. Style may be regarded as a phenomenon that will be examined as such and described accordingly; or a phenomenon that will be explained and studied accordingly. For an examination and description of the spectacular, two methods are most inviting: the 'phenomenological' method and the 'morphological' method. A work of art, a mathematical idea, a moral precept, a social institution, are facts which acquire their full meaning only as moments in the order of a conscious purposefulness. 'Style', which emerges in connection with such facts of consciousness, might be considered most suited for a phenomenological approach. However, as soon as we try to regard style, in keeping with the phenomenological methods and

From Horizon and Style (1935) 113

technique, as a moment which, through its essence, partakes of conscious purposefulness, we come against very annoying difficulties. In our opinion the style of a work of art, for example, is imprinted on the work while it is being created; but this effect is not the result of conscious purposefulness. However intentional some aspects of a work of art may be, its more profound stylistic imprint makes it a product of ultimately unconscious factors.

Therefore, by its more profound stylistic aspect, a work of art is part of an unintentional demiurgic order, not of consciousness. As a rule, the facts that can be considered in terms of style belong—by the place they hold in life—to the order of the spirit and of the mind; by other factors, which determine them from below, these facts belong to an order that is beyond consciousness. As we shall discover in this study, it is in the very *style* of the created works that the factors which are beyond consciousness find their full expression. Style as a phenomenon seems to evade the circle of light of current phenomenology inasmuch as it cannot be integrated into a conscious intentional order.

In some respects, 'style' appears as phenomenon for whose description and highlighting the morphological method offers the best chances of success. For those who are inclined to mistake phenomenology for morphology we note that morphology as it is practised does not turn the fact under consideration into an object of 'transcendental consciousness'; nor does it want to discover the essence of the fact in a purpose. Morphology studies forms as such, recorded on a staff of natural facts. Morphology introduces a plastic order in the ever-changing dynamic world of forms. Morphology does not look for unalterable, abstract, absolute essences, as phenomenology does; rather it tries, with impressive flexibility, to distinguish original, dominant forms and derived, secondary forms. A classic example of morphology: from the form 'leaf', Goethe derived all the partial forms of a plant—the root, the stem, petals, stamens, etc. In the spirit of morphology 'derived' forms often possess, as this example shows us, only a vague similarity with the supposed 'primary' form, and sometimes practically no external similarity. Thanks to its methodical plasticity and flexibility, morphology established a link between highly differentiated forms ('root', 'stem', 'petals', 'stamens'). When it must pronounce its opinion on the 'essence' of these forms (root, stem, petals, stamens), phenomenology will certainly not stop at the form 'leaf'. The 'essences' which phenomenology aims at are static and rigid, whereas the 'original phenomena' or 'primary', 'dominant' forms which morphology aims, at are dynamic and plastic. When it has to study the same facts, phenomenology will endeavour to distinguish the essential from the nonessential, which in fact does not mean very much since a normal intelligence naturally takes care of this operation. When morphology studies forms, its efforts are quite different. Morphology regards a dominant form as a 'habitus' too, among other things—that is, morphology studies this form also in terms of all its latent possibilities. And by their aspect these 'possibilities' are sometimes very remote from the dominant primary form.[1] We think that the study of possibilities is extremely useful.

In fact, phenomenology and morphology differ also in other respects. Whereas phenomenology is a purely descriptive method, sometimes set in motion in a complicated mechanism of theoretical devices, morphology is a less constrained and more freely breathing descriptive method. Unlike phenomenology, the morphological method takes a step towards the explanatory position, because it wants to uncover also the hidden side of the phenomenon under consideration.

'Style' appears partly as a unity of dominant forms, stresses and attitudes, in a rich, diverse and complex variety of forms and contents. As regards characterisation, we are convinced that morphology possesses, in a high degree, the faculty of communicating with the phenomenon of 'style'. The only unsettled question is whether morphology is really able to tell us everything that can be said about style. We believe that morphology does not exhaust the phenomenon! The phenomenon 'style' contains and implies also factors which exceed the capacity of sympathy and the grasping powers of morphology. This is due to the fact that style is made up not only of 'forms', but also of other elements, such as: horizons, stresses and attitudes. And morphology, as its name reveals, is designed mainly to put us in touch with the world of forms. Then there arise a number of questions regarding style from the explanatory point of view; morphology with its rather poor explanatory qualities, definitely remains indebted to them. Morphology will be able partly to describe the phenomenon, but it will be unable to 'explain' it. In response to a complex theoretical interest we shall often have the opportunity to cross the barriers of morphology in this work. On the descriptive and analytical plane we shall use, according to the circumstances and to the nature of the problems, all the means which have proved useful and which are available to us; on the explanatory plane we shall resort mainly to the methods and constructions of 'abyssal psychology' or the psychology of the unconscious, which we expand by adding to it a new discipline we are founding; we call it 'abyssal noology'. Abyssal noology deals with the structures of the unconscious mind (*noos, nous*), because we admit the existence of an unconscious 'mind' alongside the unconscious 'soul'. In this way we indicate the methods whose advantages we shall try to use and at the same time we circumscribe the ground on which we are going to erect the required theoretical constructs.

Translated by Georgeta Bolomey

(B) From 'The Stylistic Matrix'

Making use of so wide a range of elements, the theory of 'style' has assumed an ever more important place in Blaga's philosophy, becoming ever more pertinently meaningful. We have systematically developed a theory of style, allowing it to branch out in ways undreamed of until him and to assimilate theories, not only from psychology, aesthetics, or a certain descriptive philosophy of culture, but also from anthropology, ontology and metaphysics. To show the extent, depth and degree that the theory of style has assumed in Blaga's vision, suffice it to note he has introduced metaphysical significance to the stylistic matrix and to its components.

The stylistic matrix is an unconscious complex yet it does not operate inside the unconscious. The farthest concentric layers of signification reach out into the conscious areas of our psyche. In other words, 'the stylistic matrix' is one of those complicated, secret instances or mechanisms through which the *unconscious organises the consciousness* without the latter being aware of it.

The stylistic matrix, as we conceive it, may be considered the permanent substratum of an individual's life-long creation; it its essential elements the stylistic matrix is similar—to the point of being identical—in several individuals, in a whole people or even in a part of mankind in the same age. It is only the existence of an unconscious stylistic matrix that can explain such striking a phenomenon as the stylistic consistency of certain creations. 'Stylistic unity' is sometimes of a miraculous purity; that is, miraculous if we consider the psychological conditions in which it appears and which are inconsistent, uncertain, non-linear, kaleidoscopic and restless. Emotions and problems, upsurges and doubts, passions and hesitations, all that mass of aleatory impulses and random projects of individual consciousnesses would only form a puzzling, incoherent picture unless a solid armature, a 'stylistic matrix', were not set under them and beyond them; its patterns influence, first of all, the stylistic structure of artistic, metaphysical and cultural creations.

The stability of these patterns is indeed superlative. It is not an exaggeration, we believe, to say that such a stylistic matrix, once established in the unconscious, can stand— unaltered—any attack of the conscious. Let us suppose, for instance, that, in certain circumstances, consciousness chooses a course which no longer corresponds to the unconscious patterns consolidated in a stylistic matrix. By attentively investigating such cases, I have come to the conclusion that the unconscious stylistic matrix does not suffer too much as a result of conscious deviations. One might therefore imagine the following situation: an author deliberately chooses to follow and obey directions completely opposed to those upon which he is unconsciously fixated. The unconscious 'stylistic matrix' will continue to hallmark his creation, placing his consciousness—already turned towards other horizons, other attitudes, other accents—in front of a *fait accompli,* as it were. The constraints and the decisions of the consciousness have no power beyond the latter's limits and frontier while unconscious patterns can be readily projected into consciousness as well, directly or in disguised form (. . .). As a rule, the unconscious stylistic matrix resists any form of conscious criticism with the stubbornness of an organic defect. Most great poets still conceive their creations in an archaic, magic or mythical mode no matter how convinced they may be that in ascending to the high plateaux of consciousness they have left all such nonsense behind. When writing the psychological biography of a personality, one must always keep in mind this two-storied structure with its immanent play of perspectives. Specially to be remembered is the fact that the unconscious is infinitely less susceptible to change than the conscious. The unconscious is conservative by definition. Most often the unconscious succeeds in remaining identical to itself in its subterranean bed in spite of the lucid and critical convulsions of the consciousness. The stylistic matrix, though a spiritual reality in its own right, stands towards the consciousness in the relation in which atoms stand towards chemical methods: no matter how chemically complex, atoms cannot be altered in their structure by any chemical method.

The stylistic matrix can be seen as a general concept about which we can speculate theoretically in diverse and fruitful ways. The stylistic matrix is made up of the following elements:

1. The spatial horizon (the infinite, space-as-cupola, flat space, *Mioritic* space, alveolate [honeycombed]-sequential space);
2. The temporal horizon (time-as-fountain, time-as-cascade, time-as-stream);
3. Axiologic accents (affirmative and negative);
4. Anabasic and catabasic elements (or the neutral attitude);
5. The formative impulse (the individual, the typical, the elemental).

'The stylistic matrix' is like a packet of categories unconsciously fed into all human creations and even into human life since the latter can be moulded by the spirit too. In its categorical capacity, the stylistic matrix imprints itself, with modelling effects, upon works of art, metaphysical conceptions, scientific doctrines and theories, upon ethical and social conceptions. In this respect let us recall the fact that our 'world' is modelled not only by the categories of the conscious, but also by other categories, whose dwelling place is the unconscious. *Man's creative horizon, in relation to 'the world', is not simple as Kant and his followers believed, but multiple, or at least two-layered. 'Our world', therefore, partakes of human spontaneity with exponential intensity.*

Translated by Anda Ţeodorescu

(C) From 'The Axiological Accent'

One of the determinants of the 'phenomenon of style' and of the 'stylistic matrix' is the axiological accent, described and exemplified in the extract which follows, especially in relation to the style of Indian culture. Blaga refers in his books also to numerous other types of frameworks and cultures: Arabic, Greek, ancient Chinese, and Renaissance and 20th Century European. These cultural styles manifest local variations of a universal theme, that the human world is experienced as a field of value and disvalue.

'Style' is a very complex phenomenon calling for a very comprehensive explanation. If we stopped at the unconscious horizons as the only determining factors of this phenomenon, that would mean we were satisfied with an obviously incomplete explanation. No circumstance, no fact and no indication authorise us to choke the explicatory basis: on the contrary, all the signs invite us to broaden and deepen this problem. We have assigned to the unconscious horizons a place among the determining moments of the phenomenon in question. Horizons, however, provide only a preliminary framework in which will operate the other, not less important, factors of style. In what follows we shall be trying to open a way to the other agents on which depends the phenomenon that interests us. In the preceding we have been able to establish that the unconscious, by a kind of organic projection, builds its two horizons, the spatial and the temporal. To these horizons, once woven and cast like a net over existence, the unconscious will promptly add an 'axiological accent.' What is the meaning of this accent, and its place in our theory? The 'axiological accent' also is, primarily, the reflex of an unconscious attitude of the human mind. Although organically united with its horizons, the unconscious takes an 'evaluating' attitude and initiative towards the horizons it has adopted, to the effect that it lends them the accent of a value. You may indeed feel yourself organically united with something, but this circumstance does not oblige you to regard that something as having a positive value. Sometimes it is like this. But at other times you may feel yourself organically united with something and yet reject that something as having no value. Organic solidarity does not necessarily involve solidarity in terms of value, or on the axiological level. Examples quite at hand will confirm this. You feel organically united above all with yourself, to the effect that you cannot go outside yourself without injuring the principle of identity. But this circumstance will not oblige you to admire the embodiment of maximum values in yourself. Similarly, you may feel organically solidary with your nation, with which you become integrated through your origin and innermost dispositions, through your blood and ancestral callings. That does not necessarily mean that you value the nation as the substrate and possessor of an exclusivity and as the faultless embodiment of certain supreme ideals. This dissociation between organic solidarity and axiological-accent solidarity also operates in the field we are dealing with. In this area where we are now, thanks to the analyses we have conducted, two kinds of solidarity are indeed possible, sometimes coinciding, sometimes not. An any rate, organic solidarity and axiological solidarity 'with something' do not necessarily imply each other. Between organic solidarity with a certain horizon and axiological solidarity with the same horizon there is occasionally a parallelism, lending the spiritual attitude to existence a massive, vigorous, impressive and unequivocal aspect. At other times, however, the relationship between the two possible kinds of solidarity, assumes the aspect of a polarity, lending the spiritual attitude to existence a note that is at least paradoxical, if not strange and incomprehensible. To illustrate the fact that along with organic solidarity with a certain horizon we may find an axiological non-solidarity, Indian culture can supply a highly instructive example.

How does Indian culture appear in terms of the conceptual dissociation between 'organic solidarity' and 'axiological solidarity' as related to the structure of horizons? The answer will be enormously facilitated if we first attempt a general characterisation of Indian art and metaphysics. It must be, indeed, one without any discrimination or preconceived preferences. We shall see which aspects of Indian art and metaphysics are due to the axiological accent with which India has enriched this horizon.

The spatial horizon, with which India feels to be organically solidary, must be manifest above all in certain peculiarities of Indian art. Indian art elicits from us interest rather than enthusiasm, owing to the multitude of aspects differentiating it, almost to singularity, from art as practised elsewhere. Sculpture, relief, architecture and ornament make up—interlocking with one another more than anywhere else—a unitary, almost indivisible complex. This fact, very striking and very common, can bewilder the viewer and throw into perplexity any uninformed European. The phenomenon calls, however, for keeping our poise. Let us ignore whatever might displease us, even the promiscuity of forms and the permanent, obstinate confusion of genres, and look at everything leaving aside the code of our own standards. Indian art, predominantly of a sacred nature, is represented by an enormous abundance of monuments. We number under these categories temples, monasteries, cells for meditation, reliquary mounds, sacred enclosures with portals, symbolic columns. Indian art has, no doubt, become differentiated into several styles, depending on the period, centre and community. We are more interested in the general aspects than in the details of style. Let us dwell on what is representative, such as the purely Brahmanic temples of Elephanta (we are tempted to view Brahmanism as the purest embodiment of the Indian spirit) or the monuments at Elura, illustrative of Jainism. (In describing the monuments of Indian even terms like 'sculpture' and 'architecture' will sometimes be unsuitable.) Not less representative are the temples in Udaipur, of the Sicara type (northern style) or the Vimana towers (southern style). An altogether specific, local kind of art can be seen in the Santshi columns and portals of sacred enclosures from the springtime of Buddhism, or in the marble reliefs of the Amaravati stupa, or in the plastic, cyclical and legendary architecture of Borobudur (Java) which embodies the cosmology of the Mahayana. If we duly leave aside the too obvious Hellenistic influences and infiltrations, we can also consider the art of Gandhara, supremely refined and more directly and convincingly accessible to European sensibility. This list of representative monuments is far from complete but perhaps just sufficient to guide us approximately in a vegetation that defies any mental attempt at ordering. Regardless of the altogether local splendours and regardless on all minor stylistic differences between the monuments at various sites, Indian art in general strikes one, compared with European art, primarily by its unbounded excess, truly tropical, savage, refined and barbaric, of plastic fantasy. Only European baroque (derived in fact from a different, less erotic spirit), and only in its most prolific moments, can somehow remind us of the overwhelming and suffocating richness of India's plastic fantasy; not in style, of course, but rather as an orgy of forms. India, to the extent it can actually come in touch with our continent, must experience before European art a painful feeling of dearth of formal imagination. Judging by the code of our own sensibility, we shall in turn find that Indian art suffers from a supersaturation of forms. What comes to the fore at one's first encounter with Indian art is, besides the profusion of forms, a strange moderating compensation for this aspect: the obsessive repetition of the same motif. The richness of its plastic fantasy, hot and restless like the air the midday sun, assumes, through motif repetition, a constant, assuaging aspect of monotony. A mortifying monotony poured out over an excess of plastic forms, that is the dominant note of Indian art in all of its styles. This art grows, as if in competition with the tropical flora of the landscape. With its forest of symbols, live or withered, Indian art looks like an exuberant appendix, a play and a reflection, of the vegetation and the geological formation. The turnings of the temple of Bhuvanesvara, springing by chance, in every possible dimension, next to one another, in a magically observed disorderliness, look like huge cactuses in a world contaminated by fairy-tale logic. The sagacious elephant, the cruel tiger, the noble horse, the monkey—a caricature of human vices—and other fabulous beasts significantly intermingle with the unstable fauna of fierce or interiorised, creative or destructive deities. All is prolonged into all, limitlessly, in a universal betraying of logical precision and a general sliding into symbiotic structures. Such a characterisation may not, however, go beyond the palpable, the optical surface and evidence. The groundwork for an in-depth probing once laid, a more essential question arises: What latent spatial horizon is expressed in this art?

We invite the reader to take down any history of Indian art and look, for instance, at the column of a portal with its ornamental devices, at the hollows and marble elaborateness of a stupa, at a swollen tower of Bhubaneswar, or at a relief-tormented wall of some temple-cave on Elephanta. He will promptly notice in this art a kind of *horror vacui* which seems to have actuated its creator. The artist is almost obsessively concerned with the problem of putting some plastic content into every void of the frame at his disposal. Confronted with a wall bearing the colossal reliefs of the god Siva and his wife, Parvati, the artist felt prompted to load with agitation every empty nook and recess, and he put in, interwoven, gradually more and more diminutive figures and motifs. From the colossal size of the framework and the dominant figures the beholder's eye is thus guided, as from the arteries towards the increasingly branched veins, as from a pool to ever smaller alveoli, and eventually made to lose its way in a miniature infinity. The plastic expression has found here an infinite spatial horizon. But is this infinite horizon the same as the one found in European art? In a certain sense it is, we believe; although in Indian art the infinite perspective is somehow reversed towards its other fictitious end. The European artist proceeds by expansion, by evolution, from a certain framework towards the *great* infinite perspective (Rembrandt). In the functionalism of the structural elements of Gothic cathedrals, the lines of the vertical ecstasy, for instance, denote an excess, a pouring forth of the architectural mass into the great infinite. In India, the artist governed by the same infinite horizon decides otherwise: he starts from a frame, but makes you deepen this frame into an infinite horizon, *interior* to it. From a frame given beforehand, the European starts towards the great infinite outside: from a frame given beforehand, the Indian goes by a kind of involution towards the small infinite within the frame. The European and the Indian are in fact possessed by the same infinite horizon, but they exploit it in opposite ways and directions. In European art the original framework breathes openly in a wide, infinitely rarefied horizon; in Indian art the same original framework vibrates inwardly, in a horizon of the utmost density. The 'colossal' and the 'minute' will most often be juxtaposed within the same framework in Indian art, without any problematising or qualms of conscience. This fact redolent of nonsense and strikingly curious at first glance appears to the European as decidedly objectionable, as a 'lack of style' if not an actual monstrosity. But it is sufficiently general to deserve a more generous interpretation. The phenomenon is too common to be regarded as lack of style: it is, rather, the striking symptom of 'another' style. The phenomenon is indeed 'stylistic' *par excellence* as it helps to reveal a human procedure consistently obeyed in treating the spatial horizon. In Indian art 'the colossal' and 'the minute' do not have the signification of 'colossal' and 'minute' pure and simple; the colossal and the minute represent, in Indian art, elements of a system of artistic techniques; they are moments, stages, by which the vision of infinity is achieved in an involutional perspective. We must take into account the fact that the artist, proceeding by involution and wishing to advance from the framework towards the interior infinite, has no other solution than juxtaposing the colossal and the minute. This very normal and in no way precarious state of affairs has not been very well understood by European commentators anchored in certain optical habits. There remains, no doubt, the question why the Indian, while living in an infinite horizon as does the European, eventually chooses to treat this horizon by an opposite method. We think we are not wrong to interpret this reversal of method as resulting from an attitude of *axiological non-solidarity* with the horizon. We emphasise that the Indian, even more than the European, because of some unconscious convention, lives with all his senses and all his pores open to the infinite horizon. The Indian is organically solidary with this infinity, in a more decided way than is the European. But in his mind a *negative* axiological accent has been laid over this organic, primary solidarity with the horizon. Under the impact of this unconscious orientation, the Indian regards the spatial horizon with all its contents as a *non-value*. Consequently the artist, proceeding from a frame will no longer integrate this frame in the great infinite as does the European in keeping with his own affirmative logic. The Indian will act in the contrary direction: he will make a negative gesture and will somehow withdraw from his natural horizon—assigned to him and regarded by him as a non-value—and take the path of *involution*. The negative axiological accent laid by the Indian upon the spatial horizon has produced in art a reversing of the infinite perspective. What then distinguishes the Indian, even to the degree of singularity, is not so much the horizon as the axiological accent. A negative axiological accent will not result in annulling the horizon. The horizon persists and the negative accent overlies it only through what leads to highly complex and paradoxical aspects.

The infinite horizon, and the negative axiological accent, as unconscious agents, are even more visible through their effects, in Indian metaphysics. Indian metaphysics confirms, by the force of its formulae, what Indian art allows us but to surmise in a roundabout way. To distil the negative axiological accent from the multitude of forms found in Indian art one must make an earnest effort to understand and must use a refined exegetic technique. The meaning of the Indian perspective, with its arrow turned from the framework towards the interior infinite, has had to be brought out by a reflected interpretation, following a rather circuitous path, and by a recourse to concepts so far not employed in the theory of art, such as that of 'involution.'. In Indian metaphysics, the infinite horizon is implied as in gravel in stagnant water, and the negative axiological accent is expressed straightforwardly in a number of formulae. Things, beings, elements and divinities have always been a matter of tormenting interest to the Indian, not so much in themselves as owing to the fact that, real or imaginary, all existences and beings insert themselves—due to the manner in which they are conceived—without any resistance into a single, overwhelming infinite horizon. The Vedic shepherd carrying the seed of the Upanishads in his soul, the shepherd rushing into a sunburnt land from somewhere in the North, the shepherd who near improvised temples sang hymns to heaven, to magic and to fire, that shepherd had from the first his gaze turned into deep infinity. His insatiable imagination grasped a boundless universe, his mind rolled over a horizon without limits. His imagination, leaping from metaphor to metaphor, delighted in super proportions and indulged in breaking all limited forms. Legitimacy was denied the isolated, individual object, which found its justification only as a moment included in an unlimited principle. The large number, of astronomical proportions—as one would put it nowadays—first came to play a role in the history of human thought in the various Indian cosmogonies. Furthermore, an Indian's horizon was infinite not only in the sense of its wide unfurling: the same infinite horizon opened to him in the other direction, towards the 'small', as far as its disappearance into nothingness. Through his original spiritual substance an Indian will so strongly vibrate in an infinite horizon as to have all bounds, in every field and every direction, burst under his gaze. An Indian will expand his 'self' until it becomes the oneself of all the world. It may also happen that he will not expand it: then, under the pressure of the same infinite horizon, the Indian will multiply his self, imagining the law of Samsara, or the 'reincarnation' in countless lives. However, as a result of a great, continental disappointment, or by some secret compensatory technique of the human soul, all this infinite horizon becomes to the Indian a non-value rather than a place of redemption of desolation. The negative axiological aspect, detectable throughout Indian culture, has a variety of facets, more radical or more subdued, but it is found in all the metaphysical systems, either explicit or implicit as the leaven in the dough. Thus, in Brahmanic mysticism, as contained in the Upanishads, in that mysticism of losing one's self into a higher self which found its late crowing in the vast monistic doctrine of Sankara, the noble commentator; thus in the Samkhya dualistic system, in the Jainist doctrine of great ethical pathos, in the teaching of Buddhism—both the earlier ones and the tortuous scholasticism of the Mahayana.

1. Brahmanic mysticism accepts as existent only the absolute and impersonal principle, that is the supreme, hidden unity: Atman. From the monistic viewpoint of Brahmanic mysticism, the infinite spatial horizon is but the lure of the form of Maya, illusion, play, which an ascetic must never permit to attract or delude him. Through the negative axiological accent the organic horizon of the Indian soul acquires, in Brahmanic mysticism, the character of a cosmic illusion. The horizon is not annulled, it persists as an infinite delusion.
2. The Samkhya doctrine builds upon an initial dualism: it admits first a plurality of psychic units, and matter consisting of elements. This doctrine views matter, as an integral part of existence, in a clearly realistic way, unlike Brahmanic mysticism, according to which matter is only an illusory, reflected reality, a kind of phantasm. But the Samkhya doctrine too lays a negative accent on the spatial horizon in regarding the world of matter, if not as an illusion, at least as a non-value, which, as far as we are concerned, leads to the same axiological accent. In other words, here too we find a platform for legitimising the ascetic life: it lies in devaluing matter, in degrading it, not as reality but as a vital environment. It is more a kind of moral degradation. Man is advised to live in such a way as to contrive at any cost an escape from the entanglement of matter. The idea of salvation through mortification, through asceticism, from the yoke of

reincarnation found its earliest elaborate expression precisely in the Samkhya doctrine. ('Samkhya' is not properly a single system but, like Brahmanic mysticism, a doctrinal tenet found and variously commented on in several systems, a central flock of wool from which thinkers spin their yarns to the best of their knowledge and abilities. The Samkhya doctrine is, at least in part, the basis of Jainism and Buddhism alike, since both are concerned with the technique of salvation from the yoke of Samsara, or the law of reincarnation.)

3. Jainism has carried the teachings about 'ahimsa' to the last, almost grotesque consequences. Ahimsa is the commandment not to kill or hurt living beings in any possible way. The Jainist doctrine wants to approach the world at a tangent, although man clearly lives within the circle. This morality is impressive by its absolute respect for life: starting from it, a whole network of precepts and modes of conduct was imagined with a view to attaining individual salvation. (A Jainist, for instance, will go about with his mouth covered so as not somehow to swallow a gnat.) Existence in the spatial and temporal horizons is seen as non-value. Breaking the cycle of reincarnations is pursued as the supreme ideal and as the strategy of one's whole life. What diligence in suppressing the most natural inclination, what self-flagellation and what tortuous devices used merely to become exempt from reincarnation! And let us note the latent tension between the spiritual components of Jainism. What an amazing criss-cross of horizons and accents: absolute respect, pushed to self-sacrifice, for any kind of life, and a firm resolution to view life as a non-value!

4. The problem of breaking the cycle of reincarnations is also central to Buddhist concerns. Buddhism advances, as the method leading to this goal, mainly inward detachment from any passionate interest in one's own life, then compassion for all living beings and concern to save them all without discrimination, as all are subject to the same fatality of returning. While Brahmanic mysticism sees the infinite spatial horizon as an illusion coming from Atman, or as a meaningless play indulged in by a lonely God (the exoteric, second-hand teaching), Buddhism felt called upon to radicalise the negative accent, stating that behind the illusion of our senses and behind the idea of substance there is *nothing*. 'Nothing' as the substrate of a cosmic illusion, that is the doctrine about the bottomless river. The Buddhism of later times, flourishing in the luxuriant

scholastic teaching of the Mahayana, took yet another step towards negative radicalisation. The thinker Nagarjuna, fallen prey to an abstract nihilistic inebriation, put forward teachings about 'the empty absolute' (*sunyata*): not only is the sensible world an illusion; the fact that man thinks he exists and even the fact that man thinks he feels the sensible world are also mere illusions. The negations resolve here in a dizzy excitement without any outcome. And thus, the waters of denial completely overflow the horizons of existence.

The everyday moral standards and practices, based on the conceptions briefly described above, invariably culminate in negative asceticism, that is, is the advice—turned to actual conduct—to collaborate with no action, good or evil, of those that occur, playfully and unrestrainedly, in the infinite horizon of life.

Indian art and metaphysics, perplexingly rich in forms and thoughts, illustrate *ad oculos* that having a horizon is one thing and wrapping this horizon in a halo of a value is *another*. These are two autonomous terms, two separate forces. Indeed, two distinct factors cross or meet in the magnificent vegetation of Indian art and metaphysics, two factors overlapping not in the spirit of a reassuring parallelism, as in Europe, but in the precipitous spirit of a strange polarity. In European culture, the infinite spatial horizon is strengthened by a positive axiological buttress; in the Indian's soul the same horizon bears a negative stigma. The Indian's and the European's spatial horizons are, in a way, *synonymous*, getting a divergent meaning through the *accents* laid upon them. It is obvious that the coupling of an infinite horizon with a negative accent has lent Indian culture as a whole the note of a fascinating paradoxicality, a profound charm that calls and frightens one, an enchantment which at the same time attracts us and makes us ill at ease.

By way of conclusion we shall contend, in other words, that there may exist cultures very different in style, although growing in the atmosphere of the *same* spatial horizon. Such a thesis, flanked by the required explanations, can extinguish the credit given to a morphological conception that endows each culture with a specific space. Other factors too, not less significant than the spatial horizon—which accidentally, as we have seen, may be the common site of several cultures—can participate in differentiating the cultures. The style of a culture is not determined by the seal of a single factor. Two cultures, involving the same horizon, can still be very different, due precisely to the other factors that determine the phenomenon of style. Like the Gothic European, the Indian had an intense vision of infinity and yet, they managed to become the authors of a highly original, unique culture which is not the European culture 'once again'. The originality of the phenomenon is assured in this case by other factors rather than by the spatial vision resorted to in the morphology haunted by the mania of the single idea. One heterogeneous factor through which European culture and Indian culture become sharply differentiated is precisely the axiological accent invariably placed on the spatial horizon. To a European, the infinite horizon is the vessel of all values; to an Indian, the same infinite horizon is the vessel of all non-values.

The axiological accent should generally be viewed as an addition to the spatial horizon, as a plus and a completion. The unconscious creates its own spatial horizon just as the snail builds its calcareous shell. From the fact that the unconscious is organically solidary with the horizon it has created, it does not follow that existence in this horizon should be appreciated as such. It may easily happen that the horizon is felt as an infirmity. Indian culture convincingly illustrates this, with theoretical repercussion that must unconditionally be taken into account.

Translated by Florin Ionescu

Editors' note:

* C.F. Hebbel (1813-1863) was a German poet and dramatist

Note:

1. In our essay *The Original Phenomenon* (1925) we demonstrated that the morphological method cannot be reduced to mere 'Platonism' either. We distinguished the morphological method, and attributed to it a more dynamic and more flexible character. Platonism is static. Moreover, in that study we established that an 'original phenomenon' differs from a Platonic idea in that it has 'polar' aspects and moments. 'The leaf', the original phenomenon of vegetation according to Goethe, takes so many different forms, becoming root, stem, corolla, stamens, etc. Thanks to its polar dynamic: 'the leaf' shrinks and expands rhythmically. In the study, *The Original Phenomenon*, we actually said that, accepting the morphological method uncritically, we do not consider it suited for research in all fields. We found that the philosophy of culture is the most appropriate field for this method. This does not imply that we wanted to eliminate other methods which would lead to effective results from the philosophy of culture.

Chapter 10

From *The Mioritic Space* (1936)

From 'The Mioritic space'

The following consists of most of the first and title essay in what has proved to be Blaga's most popular philosophical work in Romania. Blaga finds primarily in traditional songs (the 'doina', mentioned below, is the traditional and melancholic form of Romanian folk song), and also in domestic architecture, manifestations of specific 'spatial horizons' or ways in which space is conceived and structured, not in the abstract, but in lived experience. ('Horizon' is used by Blaga in the extended phenomenological sense of that which delimits a form of experience, and so 'spatial horizion' is not a tautology and does not mean the visible horizon.) He argues that his theory of a 'spatial matrix', of a set of 'abyssal' or fundamental categories, of which we are not consciously aware and which shape the way in which we experience space, can explain how a given way of experiencing space, formed over centuries, can yet continue in different settings, which the simply causal theories of his predecessors could not do.

It has been said that music, being based on sonorous sequences, would have no joint of contact with the spatial horizon as the inherent properties of its substance—sound or tonality—are incompatible with spatial structures. This opinion, now a commonplace, includes a large amount of superficiality and cheap conventionalism. Let us listen to one of Bach's cantatas or 'Passions.' Let us position ourselves within the sonorous field of this music and have its lines of force project themselves, by induction, upon our mind. Still, before opening ourselves to this bewitching embrace, let us ask ourselves: In what spatial horizon does the mind expressing itself through the music exist? There is only one answer, a plain one, which anybody can give without trying too hard, just because it is the only one: in Bach's music, vibrantly and overwhelmingly expressed, there is a spatial horizon, yet one also with a specific structure: the infinite horizon, infinite in all its constituent dimensions. This type of horizon is sensed from the rhythm and the inner line of the music, just as, in their flight, birds sense the extent of space which they feel around them. There is, of course, a paradox in this statement: arts which, by their media and structures, are directly dependent on space, as are painting or architecture, fail to express this vast spatial horizon as forcefully as a Bach Passion or cantata does. The paradox is interesting for us since it points to the fact that we carry in our unconscious certain horizons which are so eager to express themselves that they use for that purpose totally alien means. The expressive virtues of music are striking in this respect.

Repeating the experiments with Bach's music on another example, one notices that the spatial horizon expressed through music is not always one and the same but varies greatly. I suppose every one of my readers has had the opportunity to hear a Russian folk-song. Let the reader listen to it once again, actually or in recollection, and, pervaded by the special nostalgia and by the echoes of despair of the song, let him ask: in what the spatial horizon, scanned within, exists the human spirit which expresses itself and its suffering in this way and through this language? It is evident that in the Russian folk-song there resounds something of the sadness of a soul that, whether it moves or stands still, feels it will never be able to reach its goal, that is, something of the heart-breaking, hopeless yearning for the unreachable. In the face of our puzzlement arises the explanation we seek: the infinite stretch of the steppe as background to and as the perspective of the Russian folk-song. Another example: we hear an Alpine song, with those gurglings as from a cascade, with those overlapping echoes, calling as from the mouths of gullies, with that spirit strong, high and earthy, rugged as a rock and as pure as a glacier. Behind such songs we can feel a spatial horizon which is theirs and only theirs: the high space of the mountain even as steep as the profile of lightning. Or again: we hear an Argentinean dance tune, one of those which have become so popular with the help of modern records. In rhythm and in velvety sound, in this song of the accordion, a melancholy takes shape; a melancholy burning in the flesh, stirred, by the sun, in the man who, in the middle of the South American pampas, waits without hope for the relaxation of an inner tension which is so great that nothing can resolve it. Here also is the expression of an inner space grown naturally and over time within a certain horizon. In the South American's soul the invincible distance of the pampas always interposes itself, it seems, between longing and fulfilment. We stress in this example not so much the impact of landscape on music, but the way that landscape integrates itself in the structure of the self, acquiring accents in this respect. Surroundings, the habitat, space therefore

From The Mioritic Space (1936) 131

live within and through the mind being specifically touched and trimmed by the latter. Let us now turn to some examples from our immediate neighbourhood. Let us now listen to one of our *doinas* with the same intention of putting into words a spiritual horizon. Now that we have become somewhat accustomed to the palmistry of hidden backgrounds, it will not be difficult to discern a specific kind of horizon also in the background of the *doina*. This horizon is: the plateau. The plateau: that is a raised, open plain, on a green coping of mountains and occasionally trickling into valleys. A *doina*–sung not in the urbanised sentimental manner of artistes in ready-made costumes nor by the suburban gypsy given to useless arabesques, but by a peasant woman or by a shepherd's wife, with a precise and economic feeling for the song and a voice expressive of the blood, which for hundreds of years has climbed mountains and scoured the valleys at the urge and command of its destiny–evokes a specific horizon: the high horizon, made rhythmic and indefinite by hill and valley.[1]

It may be objected that, as we equate a song and an horizon, we do so only to establish, what has been done so many times before, a link between music and a certain type of landscape. But this has only the function of a first approximation in defining further theses towards which we are moving. Let us therefore proceed to a number of qualifications and distinctions. We shall insist first on that in relation to what we shall do precisely, is not in the first place the expression of a landscape seen globally, but rather of an horizon in which the essence is the spatial structure as such, apart from anything else and apart from any picturesque padding, that is, of a spatial horizon and of spiritual accents which the horizon has acquired on behalf of a human destiny, a destiny constructed from a particular spirit and from a particular blood, from a particular way, from a particular suffering. We shall pursue much further the relation of which we speak and which first appears as mere correspondence between music and landscape, until it becomes revelatory for man himself and, in a certain sense, for the creative model of man.

Various reasons and circumstances suggest that we should seek the horizon which vibrates resonantly in a song, in the human mind rather than in the landscape. With this we are led to the central problem of our concern. What is heard in a song is not so much the landscape, full and concrete, of earth and rocks, of water and grasses, but first of all a space, briefly articulated by lines and stresses, somehow schematically structured, drawn in any case from the contingencies of immediate nature, a space with articulations, and vertebrate only in its essential statics and dynamics. What is the particular reason why a certain space resounds in a song? It seems to us that is only one answer can be given: a certain space vibrates in a song because it exists somewhere, and in some form, even in the spiritual substrata of the song. It remains only to be seen now how we are to visualise 'space' as a creative spiritual factor, that is, what mode of existence we are to attribute to it.

The morphology of culture (Frobenius, Spengler and others) and the history of art (Alois Riegl, Worringer), in books which represent as many monuments of insight and intuition, have striven to elucidate the role which 'the sense of space' seems to play in shaping the culture or creating a style. Frobenius anticipating, with more inspiration but more erratically, some of Spengler's ideas, pointed, in ethnology and using newly discovered material, to the relation between a specific culture and a certain sense of space. Differentiating African culture into two great blocks, Hamitic and Ethiopian, Frobenius ascribed to each of them a specific sense of space: a sense of space symbolised by the image of a domed cave for the Hamitic culture, and a sense of the infinite for the Ethiopian one. He looked upon cultures as on plants growing in the hothouse atmosphere of a certain sense of space. Spengler, in his vast and much-discussed work on the philosophy of culture, applied the same point of view to great historical cultures, distinguishing them according to the same criterion of space and separating them by an impenetrable and monadic membrane. According to Spengler, the most characteristic aspect of each culture is its specific sense of space We shall not go into details about his theory as we presume every reader to be vaguely familiar with it, if not from the original text, at least from commentaries and reviews. We shall only mention, to refresh our readers' memories and for some points of reference, the modes of the sense of space involved, according to Spengler, in some of the great cultures. Western, Faustian culture, a culture of spiritual anguish, of craving for expansion, of perspectives, involves a sense of three-dimensional, infinite space (not unlike Frobenius's Ethiopian cultures). Ancient Greek culture, Apollonian, harmonious, full of light, involves a limited, rounded space symbolised by the image of an isolated body. Arabian culture, magical, oppressively fatalistic, of the discovery of which, in all its proportions, Spengler was particularly proud, would be based on a feeling of space as domed (comparable to Frobenius' Hamitic cultures). Ancient Egyptian culture involves a sense of space as the labyrinthine way which leads to death (comparable to Alois Riegl's 'fear of space'). This theory, of 'a sense of space' defined by the above-mentioned morphologists as a function of the landscape where a culture appears, fails to satisfy us in many respects. It meets serious objections which, as it was formulated, it cannot overcome. In a previous study, *Horizon and Style,* we dealt at length on these difficulties, proposing a new theory to remove them. We spoke there about 'unconscious horizons'. We pointed out—with appropriate arguments—that the factor by which the morphology of culture or the history of art interprets as a sense of space is not, properly speaking, a sense, and even less a conscious sense, and that it is not connected with our sensibility born in a certain landscape, but is a much more profound factor. We shifted the whole problematics of space from the domain of the morphology of culture onto the plane of abyssal noology, that is, a perspective in which the unconscious is seen, not as a simple 'differential of consciousness,' but as an extremely complex reality, a reality which belongs somehow to the order of magma. This shift easily removed many difficulties. This is not the place to go into details. We shall note only that what the morphologists interpret as a sense of space as a function of a certain landscape becomes in our theory a genuine and undiluted 'spatial horizon' in the unconscious. The unconscious is not to be understood as the infinitely low level of consciousness, but as a well-structured and relatively self-sufficient psycho-spiritual reality. The 'spatial horizon' in the unconscious, existing outside and apart from external conditions and crystalised as such, preserves its identity irrespective of the variation of external landscapes. The spatial horizon in the unconscious, endowed with a fundamental structure and orchestrated by spiritual accents, must be considered a kind of necessary and unchanging frame of our unconscious mind. The unconscious exists in an organic and inseparable fusion with the spatial horizon in which it is fixed as in a shell; it is not only in a loose and changing relation, from subject to object, with this space as is consciousness in relation to landscape. Subjected to the whims of contingent circumstances, consciousness is ready to betray landscape in any moment. The unconscious does not betray. The spatial horizon in the unconscious is a deeper and more significant psycho-spiritual reality than a mere sense could ever be. To explain the stylistic unity of a culture—an impressive phenomenon in itself—we believe we cannot resort only to landscapes or feelings directly connected with landscapes. The profoundness of the phenomenon calls for an explanation involving hidden realities of a different class. Such a deep reality can be the spatial horizon in the unconscious. It can act as the determining factor for the stylistic structure of a culture or of an individual or collective mind. As we ascribe to it a determining and shaping function, we could also call it a 'spatial matrix'. There is another corollary to our theory, a fact which morphologists could not account for. This is it: there is sometimes a contradiction between the structure of the spatial horizon and the configurative structure of the landscape in which we live and in which our conscious sensibility develops. This incongruity of horizons, which can be illustrated by several historical examples, cannot be satisfactorily explained by the morphology of culture which, as we know, connects the sense of space with the structure of the landscape. Our theory about the spatial matrix as an unconscious factor can explain how sometimes, and even very often, in the one and the same landscape there can coexist cultures or minds with fundamentally different spatial horizons.

During our researches, we have often asked ourselves if one might find or construct a spatial matrix or an unconscious spatial horizon as a spiritual substratum of the anonymous creations of Romanian folk culture. The subject was worth the risk of any effort. The idea of a golden key with which to open several of the gates of the Romanian mind appeals to us. Nor is it necessary to restrict our research exclusively to Romanian folk culture. The spatial matrix, once it was hypothetically constructed, could be a window upon a whole group of people, the people in the Balkans for instance. But, of course, we are mainly interested in the Romanian phenomenon. For the time being we shall leave out the neighbouring peoples and especially the question of the extent to which these neighbours were contaminated by the spirit of the Romanian space.

The folk song, as the art that best expresses the depths of the unconscious, reveals what we have agreed to call the 'unconscious spatial horizon'. Our *doinas* have great significance in this respect, a significance which has never been sufficiently underlined. Indeed, the *doina*, with its resonances, appears as a product of perfect transparency: behind it we divine the existence of a wholly unique spatial matrix or spatial horizon. In a first approximation we have connected the *doina* with the '*plai*'* just as we have connected Russian songs with the steppe. Let us now take one step further. Let us look into the matter and its perspectives in accordance with our theory about the horizons of the unconscious. The spatial horizon

From The Mioritic Space (1936)

of the unconscious is endowed with emotional accents which the actual landscape does not possess. It is easy to identify such an emotionally coloured horizon in the *doina*: it expresses the melancholy, neither too heavy nor too light, of a heart which climbs and descends upon an indefinitely undulating plain, always moving on, again and again; or the yearning of a heart which wishes to cross the hill as an obstacle or fate, and which always has to pass over hill after hill; or the fondness of a heart which wanders under the sign of destiny which has ups and downs, rises and plunges of level, rhythmically repeated, monotonous and without end. With this spatial horizon our spirit feels itself organically and inseparably united, with this spatial matrix, indefinitely undulating, endowed with certain accents, which make of it the structure of a certain destiny. This is therefore the space that the ancestral Romanian spirit most deeply identifies itself with—and it is about this spatial horizon that we still store vague paradisaic memories in some tear-moistened corner of our hearts long after we have stopped actually living on the *plai:**

>   on a hill top green
>   a pasture of heaven...

Let us call this spatial horizon—raised and indefinitely undulating, and endowed with the specific accents of a certain sense of destiny—the Mioritic space.** This horizon, not expressed in words, can be identified in the inner structure of the *doina,* in its outer resonances and projections as well as in the atmosphere and the spirit of our ballads. However, this horizon, indefinitely undulating, results from, what is much more important, the feeling which has a sort of supremacy over the individual, ethnic or superethnic self. Here destiny is not felt as an oppressive ceiling leading one to despair; nor as a circle from which there is no escaping, but destiny is never defied with that boundless confidence in one's own powers and possibilities of expansion which can so easily become a tragic hubris. The kind of self I have in mind allows itself to be guided by a destiny with endless hills and valleys, a destiny which, symbolically speaking, descends from the uplands, culminates there and ends there. The sense of destiny deeply rooted in the Romanian self thus seems to be structured by the spatial horizon, high and endlessly undulating as it is. In fact, the spatial horizon, the unconscious and the sense of destiny, are aspects of an organic whole or elements which, once wedded, form an elastic but fundamentally inalterable crystal.

Admitting that the spirit of the Romanian people owns a fully formed spatial matrix, we shall have also to admit that, unconsciously, the Romanian lives on 'the uplands' or, more precisely, in a *Mioritic* space even when in fact and at the level of conscious perception he has been living in the plains for hundreds of years. The Romanian plains are brimming full with nostalgia for the upland. And since the lowland man cannot bring the uplands into his backyard, his soul creates its atmosphere in another way: the song is for him the substitute for uplands.

The solidarity of the Romanian soul with a Mioritic space is soft, unconscious, like a well-covered fire, not sentimentally effervescent nor consciously fascinating. This is further proof that we move there among zones of the soul's 'other world' or in the realm of investigation of the depths. These spatial affinities belong to the underground layers of our psychological and spiritual existence but they are revealed in songs and dreams. Endless rains and solitude under the stars of the uplands make our shepherd curse days he spends in company with the uplands. The shepherd's feelings, expressed in oaths like handfuls of flowers, would seem proof of his hatred of the hill top, yet, unconsciously, the shepherd remains solidary, organically solidary with this upland from which he will never try to escape. 'The Mioritic space' is part and parcel of his being. He is one with it as he is one with himself, with his blood and with his death. When he sings, this solidarity happens to come to light, as in that supreme ballad [the *Miorița*] transmitted along the centuries, in which Death on the uplands is assimilated in its tragic beauty with the ecstasy of the wedding:

> The Sun and the Moon
> Have nailed marriage to me.
> Fir-trees and sycamores
> I have wealthy guests,
> Priests, the great mountains,
> Birds, fiddlers,
> The birds, ewe-lambs,
> And the stars torches! ***

The Romanian people's characteristic sense of destiny is interpenetrated, with reciprocal plastisings and deepenings of perspective, with the Mioritic horizon. In this blend with the sense of destiny, the Mioritic space has pervaded, like an aroma, the whole of our people's life-wisdom. Pursuing our investigations in this direction, we

From The Mioritic Space (1936)

shall come across many attitudes definitely characteristic of the people's soul. Let us not lose sight even for a moment that we find ourselves in a region of nuances, of atmosphere, of the ineffable and of the imponderable. What is certain is that this spirit, a traveller under bitter-sweet stars, will neither let itself be overcome by a pitiless fatalism nor assert itself with ferocious confidence in face of the powers of nature or of chance, which he refuses to see as irreconcilable enemies. Endowed with muted acceptation on the one hand, with never excessive confidence in the other, this spirit is exactly as it should be, one which feels the road going up and going down, again and again, as if under the stimulus and in the rhythm of an eternal and cosmic *doina*, which, it seems to him, any movement must obey.

These are only a few suggestions. It now remains to see to what extent the concrete achievements of the Romanian mind, what creations and forms, reflect the indefinitely undulating structure of its space. There are various aspects which point to this effect. Let us direct our attention to the example of an aspect of the manner of siting houses. Anyone who has wandered for a day on the uplands has certainly noticed how a shepherd's dwelling stands crouched on top of such and such a hill, dominating from there right down the valley, and how, looking round, must also have noticed on the other breast of the upland another such shepherd's dwelling; something of the rhythm hill-valley has entered this system of siting. Wandering on the lowlands, we shall notice that this order and this rhythm, hill-valley, remains to some extent even in settlements on the plains, though this order appears displaced and without meaning. The houses in Romanian villages on the plain do not close up to each other in a linked, stiff and compact front, like the links of a collective unity (as can be seen in the Saxon villages), but they distance themselves, either by simple gaps or by green patches of gardens and orchards placed between houses like unstressed syllables. This distance which still remains is, it seems, the last remnant and memory of the valleys which separate the hills with the shepherds' cottages on top. It thus represents on the plains the intermittence of the valleys, as integral part of the indefinitely undulating space. Here we have an example of transposition, worth remembering and sprung from a certain spiritual constitution.

So far there is no such thing as a Romanian monumental architectural style but such a thing is not absolutely necessary in order to speak about a sense of architecture fully revealed in a small peasant cottage or in a tiny church half-submerged in grass and nettles. As regards the shape and the architecture of peasant houses we believe we can point out at least a negative but clear effect of our spatial horizon. The effect becomes apparent especially when one makes a comparison with styles that imply other horizons. It is well known, for instance, that the Russian house in the form of its architecture has a tendency to expand along a horizontal plane. As compared to a Romanian house, a Russian one wastes space. The horizontal plane encourages it to spread. Russian churches, however different in style, have one clear dimension: the horizontal; their vertical line has the uncertainty of a derivative: it is built in stages, by apses, arches and cupolas, gradually ever higher. It is also well known that western architecture, in northern countries in particular, displays an obvious tendency to expand on the vertical as if in answer to a mysterious call from above. In both cases the specific spatial horizons of the people and places intervene with their seal. Since the indefinitely undulating spatial horizon of our people thwarts expansions either horizontally or vertically, we shall define the genius of our architecture as occupying a middle position, which keeps attenuated in correct equilibrium these two opposed tendencies. The specific horizon hinders dimensional hypertrophy in a unique sense and thus intervenes, at least negatively, in the determination of architectural forms.

The metre of our folk poetry can serve as another argument, not the only one and beside the other, in favour of the thesis of the specific horizon. Our folk poetry in any case has a great liking for a metre of stressed and unstressed syllables, one by one, that is like the rhythm of hill and valley or valley and hill. This metre also displays genuine phobia for the sprightly dactyl. We think this is right, and insertions of dactyls or anapaests do not increase but disappear swallowed up by the rhythmical undulation of hill-valley which strongly runs through all our poetry as an innermost undulation. One may argue that metres composed of dactyls or anapaests are not characteristic of our language, or that such patterns would be too sophisticated for folk poetry. The last argument is not convincing since old Greek popular poetry was very familiar with those metres. The first argument, based on the specific character of the Romanian language, is no explanation, the problem only starts with it. The Romanian language must have created, probably at the same time with the building of our spatial rhythms, an interior rhythm which made it better suited for metres based on trochees and iambs than for metres based on other rhythmical unities. This interior rhythm has given the seal to our language, which it has retained ever since, a seal under the pressure of which versification inevitably adopts certain forms and refuses others. It could also be argued that the metre of hill and valley cannot reflect a specific horizon as it is to be found all over Europe. It is quite true. But the massive preference for this metre still remains as a phenomenon explicable within a specific horizon. Our songs, gracefully swaying like fields of wheat caressed by a breeze, use relatively short lines. This fact is not explained by a so-called primitivism of folk poetry in general. We refer in this respect to modern Greek folk poetry with wide-breathing lines like the sea (up to 15-16 syllables). We have in front of us a volume of original texts, with German translations, composed almost exclusively in such lines (*Neugriechische Volkslieder*, ges. V. Haxthausen, Münster, 1935). Investigators, theorists of the environment or of morphology of culture, have asked too often: What are the effects of landscape upon the human soul, and too little, what is the influence of the human soul on landscapes? A disentangling of questions is required. For one is landscape, as the starting point of a number of spiritual effects; another is the spatial matrix as an horizon of the unconscious; and something else again is that initial landscape filled, as a vessel is filled with substance, with a human sense of fate. In this last sense, the landscape is integrated into a spiritual framework. It becomes the receptacle of spiritual fulfilment; it is embodied in a sense of destiny like the wind in the sails of a ship. In this sense, the landscape is man's other cheek.

Translated by Anda Țeodorescu

Editors' Notes:

* 'Plai' means 'plateau' or 'uplands', and here refers to the landscape of Blaga's native Transylvania.

** From *Miorița*, 'The Ewe Lamb'.

***This is a literal rendering which does not retain the prosody of the original, rhyming couplets of four to seven syllables, alternating stressed and unstressed.

Note:

1. We wrote first about the undulating infinite as the specifically Romanian horizon in the magazine *Darul Vremii*, Cluj, May 1930.

Chapter 11

Aphorisms

From Stones for my temple, 1919

Moral laws change with both place and time. Some people find in that a reason not to obey any.

As regards 'ethical duties,' indeed we manage to treat our neighbour as we do ourselves: I mean, however egocentric we may be, we forget the great duties to ourselves as we forget those we have to others.

Some very profound spirits are at the same time so clear that—like the bed of a crystal-clear stream—they seem shallower than they are.

For most people 'mystery' becomes 'natural' not because they come to understand it, but because they get used to it.

Sorrow is not the only thing that may mar your happiness: somebody else's happiness may do it too.

Sometimes our duty to a genuine mystery is not to clarify it, but to deepen it so much as to turn it into an even greater mystery.

There are deep things which in the light of art can be understood more clearly than in the light of science. They say that the water of some seas is more transparent in the light of the moon than in that of the sun.

When you hate somebody ask yourself whether there is sense in your hatred; but when you love somebody don't ask if there is any sense in your love.

Our feelings also grow and grow old. Today we love and hate beings, the world, things, in another way than we did yesterday. Some feelings that we experience but rarely remain children, so to say, and fail to develop. For instance, our *amazement*, precisely because we are so seldom offered an opportunity to be amazed, is so fresh and childish. Quite often I discover within myself feelings which I have not had since I was a child—and if I take a closer look at them, I notice these feelings are as naive as they used to be at the time.

So many trees, which ruthless winds cannot break, do break under the load of their own fruit.

The fact that all lives on earth end in death could hardly prove that death is the aim of life.

The world always seems to me so new that I feel inclined to believe it occurs again and again in my soul every day: very much as Heraclitus thought the sun was reborn every morning out of the haze above sea-water.

We can see a thing clearly and plastically only if it has shades and half-shades: death is the shade that leads life plasticity.

Those who have surveyed the history of the questions that the human mind has asked itself, have certainly been able to note that the 'mystery', the 'enigma' which remove out of a question, out of a thing—are bound to appear elsewhere. The better we explain several enigmas through a phenomenon or a law, the more enigmatic do the latter become: in this matter, I should be inclined to speak about a 'principle of the conversion of enigmas.'

To the pressure of the past we have got used as we have to the pressure of the atmosphere: we could hardly exist without it.

The first aspiration of a new movement fighting against tradition is to secure a tradition.

What the Bible says—that God has made man in his image, after his likeness—hardly means that God is a man in heaven; it means that man is a God on earth.

There are many blind people—how many of them have been blinded by too much light?

When you are on earth you can either stay where you are or advance, at will; but when you fly you can only advance.

Logic suffers from a great vice of logic: it believes reality itself to be logical. If it comes up against something that cannot be understood logically, it will maintain that such something does not exist, that it is mere appearance.

That truth may also have disastrous influence upon us does not disprove its ideal value, it only proves our weakness: we are like the sick who cannot stand the fresh, brisk air of the mountains.

From The Discobolus, 1945

Know thyself: That is perfectly all right, but in order to begin something in life you ought not to wait until you know yourself. Otherwise your motto might turn into your epitaph.

Hormonal lyricism: If frank, direct and passionate lyricism were true poetry, then the stags' bellowing at certain hours of Autumn would render all anthologies useless.

On intelligence: Through its very nature, intelligence indulges in the state of infinite arguments. Evidence fills it with aversion. In front of evidence intelligence feels not only disarmed, but divested of its very nature.

Binding and unbinding: A philosophical doctrine is a prolonged and insistent invitation, made to its patrons, to take on oath on its formulae. It wants to 'bind'. But what is truly reassuring may is a doctrine in which you can also find formulae unbinding you from an oath to which you have nearly consented.

The origin of man: When a radical break occurs between an animal and the environment for which it was born, the former has only one chance of salvation: to turn into man. But this fairy-tale has only been successful once.

Selfishness as an example: Thou shalt love thy neighbour as thyself. Strange enough: in this commandment of unselfish morality, selfishness is proposed as an example to be followed, as a model, as a measure of things.

I am the freest of all my followers: To my metaphysical theories I have never ascribed any other value than that of attempts, perspectives, anticipations, mythical visions, not in any way dogmas. I have the ambition of being the freest of all followers of these theories.

Modalities of admiration: To admire a poet means to accept also his work as such. But to admire a thinker does not mean to accept also his ideas as such.

One-way traffic: One-way signs may regulate mechanical traffic in the streets, though not the circulation of saps inside an organism or that of aromas and ineffable elements within a landscape of the spirit.

Precocious virtuosity: Excessive virtuosity in a young poet or artist is never auspicious, because it is conditioned by a substantial minimum. At dawn, as a matter of fact, stars can be seen all the clearer as the greater drought is forecast.

Similarity does not necessarily imply filiation: History records so many very similar appearances – particularly on the spiritual plane, between which there is no filiation, however. Today's lightning is in no way the son of yesterday's flash.

Destiny: Our inclination to believe in destiny is strengthened by the vanity not to believe ourselves entirely ignored by the rest of the universe.

Abusive existence: There are people who—for fear of some kind of abuse—prefer not to do anything. One may say about them that their mere existence is abusive.

From The Élan of the Island, 1946

Attempt at definition: The 'real' is the possibility which for some indeterminate time turns all other possibilities into impossibilities.

Virtualities: Virtually speaking any ideal is a remorse.

In front of the poet: In front of a new, genuine poet, you always experience the paradoxical and wonderful feeling that all of a sudden you understand a language so far unknown to you.

The adulterating dimension: Seen penetratingly, reality ceases to be likely.

Nature, body, soul: In nature, our soul is more easily integrated than our body, although the latter is consubstantial with nature, while the former is not.

Hitting the right means: In order to break a ray of light, it is not enough to use the strength of your arms, or the power of all factories and mills throughout the earth, or even all mechanical powers in the universe, for that matter. And yet a dewdrop will prove amply sufficient for it.

Secret illness: In its youth genius suffers from secret old age, in its old age from secret youth.

Plagiarising nature: The birds which—as an ancient anecdote, has it—swooped upon a picture of some cherries made by a painter merely wanted noisily to denounce plagiarism, not at all to clap their wings in applause for great work of art.

Shadows: Indeed shadows resemble darkness, yet they are the daughters of light.

Discrimination: Classicism deprived of any romantic element is no classicism, but academism.

The reverse of autonomy: An autonomous cell in an organism is an incipient cancer.

Biology and cosmography: Man is the only animal that walks on two legs, vertically: he may be considered a prolongation of the earth's radius. All other animals are but tangents.

Prometheus: Man invented fire, yet he disparages himself by imagining that he stole it.

Dusk and dawn: The decadence of a spiritual epoch is never jut decadence, but also the beginning of a new epoch. While in the chronicle of nature dusk and dawn are phenomena of discontinuous succession, in the chronicle of the spirit they coincide.

Unleashing and success: Man began scoring amazing success in nature, and subduing the sky and the earth, only when he ceased believing that all things were subservient to him through their very mission and when he alone, man, declassed himself, by leaving the centre.

Man and his downfalls: How fast does man become a slave to his own creation! But in fact it was predictable that he who used to be the slave of the gods would some day become the slave of machines.

The limits of simulation: One may simulate with some degree of consistency a passion, a defect, illness, health, industry, generosity, energy—though not intelligence.

Philosophical cognition: 'Philosophical cognition' (*cunoștință*) is the one which brings about not only higher knowledge (*cunoștințe|*) but also higher consciousness (*conștiință*).*

Ideas and their cruelties: I am tried by some doubt and amazement at people ready to suffer for an idea, even unto martyrdom, for—in most cases—the same people, under different circumstances, prove inclined to impose their ideas through any means, even crime.

About a secret of poetry: It has been said that poetry is an art of words. But poetry is an art of words only to the extent to which it is also an art of non-words. Indeed, silence ought to be omnipresent in poetry, very much as death is forever present in life.

Alienation and retrieval: When you are alone too long, you become estranged even to yourself. You retrieve yourself, becoming more familiar to your own being, when you are in the presence of others.

An anvil gradually acquires the hardness of all hammers that have struck it.

The lawmaker must regulate not the spirit of submission, but the spirit of freedom abiding in humans.

The ratio between 'truth' and 'freedom:' As long as we are not masters of 'absolute truth', all individuals are entitled to the creative freedom of seeking it, each in his own way.

Thousands of years after he has ceased 'believing' in myths, man will continue speaking in terms of myths.

A 'word' resonates not only with its meaning, but with the entire universe, like the sea in a cowrie shell.

A man of culture, 'a cultured man', is he who—with his own powers or others—keeps turning chaos into the cosmos.

Those who in order to live need a theory of living, those who in order to be enthused need a theory of enthusiasm, those who in order to become passionate need a theory of passion, those who in order to exist need a theory of existence—ought to leave living, enthusiasm, passion, existence in the hands of others.

When you specialise in a certain science, you must by all means learn history too. This will heal you of any dogmatism.

Why does the sky clear up so finely after a heavy and fertile rain? In order to show that it is greater joy to give than to receive.

The kind of wisdom which denies the follies of life is neither valid nor alive. Wisdom must include folly in some way or another. Wisdom is either this or nothing at all.

It is so strange that all critics of my philosophy combat ideas which I myself have combated.

Translated by Andrei Bantaş

Editor's note:

*_Conștiință_, 'consciousness', can also mean 'conscience' in its modern meaning.

Glossary

Abyssal or stylistic categories: Lucian Blaga holds that there exist abyssal or stylistic categories that model men's cognitive and culture-creating activities. Around the year 1930, Blaga observed that there exists a level of constructional modelling by means of the categories of style, and that this level is not determined by practical experience, nor is it affected by learning processes. The categories of spontaneity, distinguished from the Kantian categories of receptivity by the level on which they occur, by their structure and function, are themselves *a priori*, hence innate. Blaga shows that former philosophies had dwelt especially on the categories of knowledge and sometimes, in a confused manner, on those of the value of good, of the beautiful, of truth. There is, however, a set of categories pertaining to the order and finality of our spontaneity. They occur on the level of the unconscious and reach the conscious only under special circumstances. It is these categories that all cultural creations are rooted in, that is to say, they underlie the cosmos factors also bear upon the way in which the categories of knowledge work, being, however, determinant for the categories of spontaneity. Thus the idea, put forth by the supporters of morphological theories on culture, *about the variability of stylistic horizons* in which a certain culture (comprising art, religion, as well as philosophy and science) is emerging acquires with Blaga an original position. There is no longer an absolute determination through one single factor (space); there is a set of categories which in Lucian Blaga's opinion belong to the style of thinking and act together with Kant's categories, constituting a second censorship of spirituality at a *space-time, behavioural and formative level*. This set comprises the horizon of prospective categories: *space* categories – (finite, sphere, infinite, undulated space, alveolar space, flat space); *temporal* categories (time as a spout, time as a cascade, time as a river); *categories* of atmosphere (affirmation, negation, neutrality); categories of orientation (anabasis, catabasis, standstill); formative categories (individual, typical, elemental). (A.B.)

Aeon: A new long-lasting paradigm or pattern of spiritual world.

Anabasic-catabasic: This meaning, understood as a course within a spatial horizon, is the seed breeding the feeling that an individual or a community has towards its destiny. This can be interpret in two different ways: as advance or progress, within the specific horizon or as withdrawal. There exists then an anabasic and a catabasic sense in the destiny of culture. For instance, the European spirit is anabasic: it is constantly advancing in its infinite horizon in an almost aggressive development which seems an endless expedition or conquest. The Hindu spirit is catabasic, in withdrawal within its own horizon, which is visible in the Hindu morals, metaphysics and art. The ancient Egyptians also had a catabasic attitude. In a way, they illustrated the definition given by Heidegger to the human being: 'an existence for a death'. What Alois Riegl called 'timidity in space', Blaga interprets as the catabasic feeling of destiny.

The man of the Mioritic space is in a constant balance in the undulating infinite of his space. He perceives his destiny as an eternal and rhythmical going up and down. (H.V.)

Creative destiny and culture as ontological mutation: Man alone has a creative destiny which modifies and even changes biological laws. This creative destiny produces a new mode of existence in the Universe—culture. Blaga defined culture as on ontological mutation. The concept of *culture* seems to have been considered by him as sufficient for expressing the essence of the human problem: culture is a more of arranging the universe through 'stylization', competing reality itself through the 'cosmoid' character of creation. Within his own limits man turns out to be a real demiurge.

But regarding the problem terms of *creation* rather than of *cognition*, with Blaga, man's dignity increases, and to the same extent increases the stress on the Great Anonym's 'daimonic' nature.

According to the Romanian philosopher, most philosophical creations, even the 'rationalist' ones, involve a certain intervention of 'mythical thinking' through the summarising condition of the philosophical concept. Therefore, it would seem wiser to set up, from the very beginning, such a mythological instance, as a kind of frame of the philosophical picture, in order to avoid a surreptitious, unwanted penetration, later on, of the mythical language in other moments of the philosophical discourse. On the other hand, myth allows the philosopher to venture (at least intuitively) also into such zones where reason, as Kant showed, is lost in antinomies. (I.G.)

The Divine Revelation: Lucian Blaga accepts both the natural revelation and the divine revelation which he conceives as 'an invasion of the human consciousness by the Divinity, as a theogonic process taking place within man'. Balga says that 'any possible surging or positive appearance of an existential mystery into the light cone of individuated knowledge is a revelation'. The revelation means 'appearance', 'the throwing of the light of consciousness'. Blaga does not accept the existence of adequate revelation. Actually, there are only dissimulating revelations. An existential mystery revealing itself to knowledge is *dissimulated* by the very structure imprinted in the human knowledge. Human being can never have an *absolute* vision. The knowledge permitted to man seems to be rather 'censored' by a *transcendent initiative,* and the revelations man alone is called upon to make seem to be rather 'braked' in a structural manner on the same transcendent initiative. In other words, man bears all the stigmata of a preventive isolation in the relationship with the absolute. Without this, man would become an unimaginable source of threats to the order of the world. That is why all religious myths and symbols should be deemed as *human* attempts to reveal the divine mysteries, as repressed transcendent attempts.

Studying the attitude of the Christian spirit towards transcendence, Blaga shows that the *transcendent* is not conceived identically everywhere and always, although its formulation from a dogmatic angle does not differ essentially. In man's attitude to transcendence there is an element of a stylistic nature generating a remarkable differentiation of outlooks which Blaga analyses from the position of a genuine comparative psychology of Christian cults. Blaga focuses his psychological considerations on three styles of Christian architecture: the Roman-basilican one, the Gothic one and the Byzantine one. The secret gist of any of these architectural modes can be interpreted both metaphysically and metapsychically. (I.M.)

Dogma: We see, in dogma Blaga, notes, more than the need for synthesis, the tendency to defend the metaphysical mystery from any attempt at rationalisation of the human spirit. No doubt, dogmas have brought about a synthetic poise without making mystery rational. Dogmas did not penetrate the consciousness of time because they were synthesis but because they were also dogmas, formulas that do not rationalise but only solve and articulate metaphysical mystery as mystery. This huge, sustained and consistent spiritual appetite, channelled unto a dogmatic direction, characterises an entire historical era and gives it a definite physiognomy.

According to Blaga, dogmas, definitely separated from their theological substratum, are antinomy transfigured by the very mystery it expresses. In conformity with this point of view, a dogma is not only antilogical but also metalogical. The simple fact that patristic philosophy itself, founded on dogmatic cognition, has been able to legitimise 'the dogmatic aeon' enables us to believe that such could emerge again, anytime in history, in order to inspire new spiritual attitudes. First Blaga shows that scientific knowledge also makes use of methods similar to the dogmatic formulas and thinking (Blaga mentions in this sense the Aleph symbol of Cantor, 'a transfinite measure which remains identical with itself no matter what finite measure would be deducted from it', comparable therefore with the dogma 'God is one and multiple'.

Ecstatic rationalism: Blaga defines as enstatic the logical modality of the intellect's behaviour, and ecstatic the metalogical modality. The intellect chooses ecstasis when all the enstatic means of dialectical thinking have been exhausted. Therefore, ecstasis implies the exhaustion of enstasis. It is a new means of cognition, another dimension of cognition which could found another dogmatic eon, regarded not as an invalidation of reasonable and logical cognition, but as a recourse, *in extremis*, to metalogics based on mythical thinking.

It is indeed sufficient to think of the subjectivism emanating from the principles enounced by contemporary physicists and epistemologists in order to consider correctly the unity between man and cosmos, seen through all its metaphysical ipseities. The first conclusion we could adopt the very moment we accept, on the one hand, the non-rationalist perspective deemed incomplete and not false, and on the other, a macro and microcosmic world, superposed by complementarity, faithful to Blaga's thinking, would involve our sudden capacity to approach a new epistemological behaviour. A non-Cartesian reason can be part of a vision of the world, similar to religion which, in the very dogmatic sense of the word and even in its most essential meaning can accept reason as a valuable way of cognition. Planck and Heisenberg were the first to accept the Christian tradition as a refusal of Cartesian separation. Blaga philosophy is an 'ec-static rationalism', that is to say a rationalism sufficiently comprehensive to spread its authority over operations classical reason never bothered with. (B.M.)

Great Anonym: The myth of the Great Anonym represents the metaphysical image of the human paradox according to which cognition and creation cannot be dissociated from certain tragical meanings. Blaga's Great Anonym is in fact similar to what the Absolute means in philosophy, this time however having a personalised anthrophomorphic form, a daimonic character which result from the defence, uniqueness against the uniqueness of man. The Great Anonym removes man's possible creative competition, instituting a 'transcendental censorship', which lowers human creation to a secondary condition. *Mutatis mutandis*, the Great Anonym is closely related to *Intellectus archetypus*, opposed by Kant to *Intellectus ectypus*, described as limited and discursive, therefore specifically human (I.G.)

Intropathy: Analysing the *subjective finality of the magical idea*, Lucian Blaga refers to *intropathy (Einfühlung)* as a tendency of the subject to 'animate' the object. There is, for instance, an animation verging on the 'personification' of a phenomenon (thunder believed to be the noise made by Elijah's chariot) and there is a more unilateral animation: for instance, the rise of the vertical in Gothic architecture is considered as a surge to the sky (upward transcendence). Man's psyche animates the object because thereby it somehow intensifies its own nature. *'Animating' the object, the soul animates itself, that is, it enhances its substance, vitalises itself* (it is a kind of *self-induction*). A world with things carrying magical loads and which therefore behaves according to some sort of laws of the soul, is, spiritually, more animate, more familiar, to us than a world which manifests only in compliance with the mechanical, physical, mathematical laws. (I.M.)

The law of non-transponibility: tends to circumscribe specific nature of the artistic aesthetic not by relation with other value projection than those in the fields of the aesthetic. Hence, the tendency to differentiate the artistic aesthetic inside the aesthetic itself, namely in its relation with the natural aesthetic. It lays down that the objective structures of the natural aesthetic cannot be transposed exactly into art without losing their initial quality, and vice versa: the objective structures of the artistic aesthetic cannot be transposed exactly into nature without losing their initial quality. We will ignore here the old habit of metaphysics of uttering laws frequently, of establishing excessive principles. This is custom is incorrect since the play of fiction, tenaciously improvising – another specific trait of art – does not, by its nature, accept laws. In Blaga's case, the claim to launch a 'law' must be granted extenuating circumstances, motivated by the very imperious necessity to render autonomous the specific nature of the artistic aesthetic. 'It is our intention here, in this chapter, and in the following, Blaga notes, to defend the total autonomy of 'artistic aesthetic', a matter that has yet been dealt with adequately, with the implied theoretical instruments.' What could have happened so seriously in connection with the specific nature of the artistic aesthetic that Blaga should have felt the need to coin a law? (G.S.)

Luciferian knowledge: Blaga establishes that our mind often permits itself singular licences and indulges in operations which form a veritable defiance to Aristotle's logic being condemned by him without appeal. Blaga proposes to attribute these operations to a new mode of knowledge, to an illogical or extra-logical mode. Thus it is that beside the 'paradisiac knowledge', which is none other than Aristotelian reason based upon identity, our philosopher installs a 'Luciferian Knowledge', full of doubts and uncertainties, but fit to fill the gaps in the other. This new mode of knowledge gives itself a new object to explore: the mysterious.

Setting out from this orientation, Blaga established an essential difference between paradisiac cognition, related to the object of cognition and self-sufficient, and Luciferian cognition, which is also oriented towards the object but detached from it. For Luciferian cognition, the object, divided into a part that is shown (phanic) and another that is hidden (cryptic) becomes a mystery. The specific moments of Luciferian cognition are the crisis of the object', the 'problematic' and 'the theoretical construction' that open up for this type of cognition the avenue of crisis, adventure, unrest and failure. So far, theorists have spoken only of a single modality of cognition, endowed almost with two nuances or gradual variants: naive cognition and civilised cognition. The difference established by Blaga between paradisiac and Luciferian cognition turn these variants into a type of polarity. Mystery, now turned notion, will become the cornerstone of a new theory of cognition; the philosopher is well aware that beyond the gates he is opening myth begins. Thus, if paradisiac cognition allows us to feel that, in a way, we have attained the world of Grace, Luciferian cognition enables us to guess the presence of a huge tragedy in which we participate without having had, so far, the chance to understand and explain it. (V.B.)

Minus cognition: means neither a lack of knowledge nor a harmless label stuck on all the mistakes of cognition, but, instead, a type of cognition conducted in a direction somehow contrary to the usual one, cognition capable of progress and unforeseeable motion ahead. The minus-cognition formulas go from a minimum of incomprehensibility to a maximum of incomprehensibility, which is seen as an abstract build-up, with no correspondence in the factual world. Minus cognition is not anti-logic but meta-logic; it does not deny, but, on the contrary, it delineates logical perception. It expands the unknown by defining formulas; therefore, this kind of cognition is properly named minus-cognition, as against the plus-cognition which curtails the unknown. Blaga claims: It is worth observing that, due to the quantum theory, modern physics affirms the antinomic structure of light: the phenomenon of light is perceived as being an 'undulation' as well as something 'corpuscular', which is a logically incomprehensible paradox. Still, some experiences necessarily demand this antinomic solution. This is why modern physics is subject to a crisis, Blaga believes that he has succeeded in demonstrating that this undular-corpuscular theory of light's nature is actually *part of a* **sui generis** *type of knowledge, that he called 'minus-knowledge'. It is not a crisis of modern physics but a new type of knowledge* that we're dealing with. We already know that Kant built a theory of knowledge that was actually meant philosophically to justify Newton's classical physics. Newton's physics only represents a particular case for modern physics. Thus, the necessity for philosophically justifying new constructions in physics by means of a new theory of knowledge, is imperative. This is, essentially, what Blaga tried to achieve in *The Dogmatic Aeon and Luciferian Knowledge* especially, by providing the theory of knowledge with the concept of 'direction'. Knowledge has not, the belief is since Kant, a unique direction (plus), to 'attenuate' mysteries, by means of a infinite theoretical process; knowledge has two opposite directions that is, plus and minus. And there are circumstances when the 'minus' direction, is required that does not attenuate a mystery, but, on the contrary, intensifies and radicalises it, rendering it in formulas exclusively antinomic.

***Mioritic space*:** To illustrate this theory, Blaga evokes a host of examples, among which the Romanian, which he develops throughout his *'Mioritic' Space*. The spatial symbol, which best represents Romanian specificity, a gently undulated plain equidistant from the steppe and the summits, and very characteristic of the Carpatho-Danubian soil. It is in this type of region that most of the popular ballads evolved, beginning with *Miorița (The Ewe Lamb)*, a veritable epic of the aboriginal peasant grappling with destiny and death. Upon local architecture, which avoids shooting upward as well as widening out; upon the peasant chant, that *doina*, where nostalgia and rapture ineffably interweave; upon popular metrics, which seek the trochee and iambus and flee the dactyl and anapaest; upon Romanian history itself, where retreats and advances rhythmically succeed one another; upon the sentiment of destiny which, with Romanians, incessantly balances between confidence and resignation; upon peasant art which betrays a constant taste for elementary and geometric forms, but tempered by the contrary taste for the picturesque, the human, the organic; we can discover the Romanian aptitude for constructing an integral and coherent world vision. Undulation, harmony of heaven and earth, of the eternal and the ephemeral; elementary representation of existence, resulting from a synthesis of geometrical stylisation and concrete picturesqueness: such are the potentials of the subconscious which engender the Romanian 'style', the Mioritic matrix. (B.M.)

Mystery: Despairing ever to attain it, orthodox reason sweeps it aside with a gesture. A too hasty gesture, according to Blaga. If, indeed, we can get no hold upon the unknowable in terms of itself, yet it does permit of being bound within the formulae of antinomies, insoluble in concrete logic. At once its formless block begins to take shape —a superhuman shape— and to glow inside with a supernatural light. Little by little, it reveals qualitative differences which permit the introduction of a scale of values and the submitting of it to the operations of conversion and classification. Whereas the logical intelligence tends to convert the mysterious into non-mysterious, by an action in a way horizontal, and to extend its empire over the surface of things, the Luciferian intelligence, on the contrary, proceeds vertically, tending to sound the mysterious, to maintain it in a state of crisis, to substitute for an absurd formula, a formula even more absurd. On the whole, it is a matter of knowledge in reverse, a 'minus-knowledge'. (B.M.)

Personance: For Blaga the unconscious becomes an autonomous factor, endowed with a cosmotic nature (an adjective derived from cosmos, and chaotic, from chaos). Blaga invalidates the theories of modern psychologists according to whom the relationships between the conscious and the unconscious is similar to the mythological relation between cosmos and chaos, and who call 'sublimation' the purifying translation of the detritus stored by the unconscious into a state of consciousness (in this sense, the unconscious would be sort of agent causing chaos). He coins the term 'personance' (from the Latin *per-sonare*) in order to better define the trait of the unconscious to penetrate and to convey its structures to consciousness. Personance would therefore be a constant phenomenon, manifest especially in the process of artistic creation during which, the unconscious, making use of the personance, explodes into the consciousness certain 'secret horizons' apt to explain a culture. Blaga resumes the great romantic tradition, adding new consistent forms and structures which the contemporary psychologists, removed from the correct metaphysical direction, have not managed to discover. To sublimation, which provides disguised realities to the consciousness, Blaga adds a second process called personance, which brings to the consciousness elements of the subconscious, echoes that are often barely perceptible but never distorted.

Revelatory metaphor: Blaga extends the significance of metaphor from manufactory metaphors to revelatory metaphors.

Manufactory metaphors are produced by putting together two more or less similar facts, both belonging to the given, imagined, experienced or apprehended world.

The revelatory metaphors increase the signification of the very objects they refer to. Revelatory metaphors bring to light something hidden, something concerning the very facts they concentrate upon. Revelatory metaphors try, in fact, to reveal a 'mystery' by the means put at our disposal by the concrete world, by the experience of the senses and by the imaginary world.

Revelatory metaphors result from the specifically human mode of existing, they are the first symptoms of this specific mode of existence, the existence of an anthropologic level, a deep level given to man together with his being. (A.B.)

Spatial horizon: The morphological theory has the creative act deriving from spatial intuition, situated in the province of consciousness. The morphologists seem to depart from Kant since they start from different data. Indeed, for Kant, space is an absolute and constant *a priori* of human intuition; for Frobenius and Spengler space is a creative act of sensitivity, that varies from one culture to another. Nonetheless, the two theories rely on the same foundations: the variable intuition of space is to be found in the consciousness. In contrast, for Blaga, the subconscious has its own horizons, entirely different from those of consciousness, and the subconscious is the one to endow space and time with determined forms, in contrast with the whimsical plasticity characterising time and space in point of conscious sensitivity. In other words, the subconscious has its own forms of intuition and the spatial horizons. (B.M.)

Style: The real dimensions of a 'style' belong to an entirely different domain than that of the sensible and the conscious: they belong to the 'abyssal' categories of the subconscious and it is by way of these that their study may be properly approached.

Thus, the theory of 'style' implies a theory of the subconscious. Freud and the psycho-analysts have treated the subconscious as function of the conscious and transported the clear categories of the latter within the obscurity of the former. Far from representing a laboratory for the conscious and nothing else, the subconscious in reality forms a world apart, the result of an adaptation where millennial experiences have dissolved, a world gifted with a personality and a life of its very own and with faculties which, though operating by seemingly occult means, nevertheless show themselves to be extremely active. Indeed, the subconscious possesses its 'spatial horizons', its 'temporal horizons' and a host of other categories, of which the conscious furnishes but the positive replica, superficial and crude; it introduces a hierarchical unity and an order of values into these categories; finally, taking position opposite destiny, it advances to the attack, resigns itself to retreat, holds its positions. But the clearest, of its initiatives is summed up in a 'formative will', which it stamps upon every human work and which determines before all else of the 'styles'. Translating the very substance of the subconscious, style appears as the organic expression of a veritable abyssal symphony, whose complex play alone can account for the infinite possibilities of the creative spirit and the thousand nuances which determine the oneness of every creation. (B.M.)

Stylistic field: Science comprises a constructional part in which theory is determined by the 'force lines' of a stylistic field. The values guiding man to knowledge are truth, verity; the definition of truth itself as positive adequacy of a content of knowledge to the content of the real is actually only a desideratum. Around the year 1930, Blaga observed that there exists a level of constructional modelling by means of the categories of style. The categories of variability, spontaneity, distinguished from the universal Kantian categories of receptivity by their structure and function. Through the spatial and temporal behavioural, formative force lines, Blaga has introduced a kind of hidden parameter, a kind of invariant capable of turning the visible complexity of cultural phenomena into an simplified pattern in an intelligible manner. He was looking for some regular spatio-temporal structures among appearances of an overwhelming diversity and succeeded in giving an outline in the history of science of the types of stylistic field peculiar to the Sumerian-Babylonian, Greek, Indian, and European culture. There are patterns of by scientific thinking, constructional ideas, controlled observations and false problems even, intimately relating to the pattern of the categories of style. (A.B.)

Stylistic matrix: Blaga calls 'stylistic matrix' the subconscious complex that determines the style of life and creation of an individual or a community, a complex of which the meaning is not exhausted between the limits of the subconscious but is completed and perfected in the area of the consciousness. 'The stylistic matrix' is hidden within those moments and secret devices which 'the unconscious administers consciousness' without the latter's knowledge. It represents the permanent substratum of an individual's whole life or of a people and it is only through it that the impressive stylistic unity of some creations can be accounted for. Once settled in the subconscious, it bears unaltered all the attacks consciousness mounts against. A man's life can be perfectly divided into two, not in the sense that it is divided for a schizophrenic, but containing a conscious life, endowed with characters, accents and modalities, often opposed to unconscious life, the penetrations or personances of which influence the work or attitude of a man. In point of consciousness, many poets have rid themselves of archaic, mythical or magic forms, yet their works continues to be thought with the help of what was apparently submerged or annihilated. The subconscious is conservatory and it happens to maintain its identity with itself in a subterranean shelter, despite the critical convulsions of the consciousness. (V.B.)

Theoric idea: The new idea thus appears as a 'bridge towards the cryptic' (as an apprehension of essences) in a *theoric* (paradigmatic) kind of thinking. The mechanist idea, Blaga says, is a *theoric* idea by which Newton opened the horizon of a *mystery*. It proposed theoretical constructions for the qualitative attenuation of the open *mystery*. More often than not the *theoric* idea carries weight in the structural joints of Luciferian knowledge even when it is dismissed later on (see the idea of the phlogiston). The *theoric* (paradigmatic) function can be fulfilled by a principle, a law, a category, a concept, a scheme. The achievability of *theoric* in one more of the problems mentioned by Blaga represents something similar to the capacity of scientific paradigm and its scope of applicability, as imagined by Kuhn.

The act of opening the mystery repeats itself indefinitely because every time the action of *theoric idea* (the paradigmatic idea) on the cryptic (the essence of thinking) creates a closed horizon of cognition, and for this reason it operates in stages. In the three phases of the problem the query, the passage to the solution and the solution Blaga describes a process that can be numbered now among the significant epistemological theories on the evolution of science. (A.B.)

Transcendental censure: This prevents the subject from penetrating mysteries. By creating the transcendental censure, the Great Anonym instills into individuated cognition the dynamic tendency of constant self-emulation; absolute individuated cognition could be dangerous for the individual for it would destroy his equilibrium as well as for the object of cognition for this could be equally created and destroyed, according to of an omnipotent subject. Such a cognition would be a danger for the Great Anonym himself whose power would be reduced and whose intentions would be thwarted by a subject that would be his equal.

If God or the Great Anonym reveals sometime his substance, it is only a dissimulation since individuated cognition, sure of the purity of the revelation, is always confronted only with what Blaga calls the illusion of adequacy, deemed a final and supreme defence measure within the transcendental censure. (V.B.)

Transfigured antinomy: The change in the time-space specificity implies a variation of the logic of identity. Lucian Blaga notices that in science there is a difference between the equivalents of transfigured antinomy and the antinomy itself. With good reason, the Romanian philosopher stresses that there is a type of specific cogitation which maintains the intellect on the field of irreconcilable contradictions and does not allow 'the outflow of the mind into the colourless matrix of the a-categorial singleness'; he calls this type of dogmatic cognition as a transfigured antinomy, a minus-cognition, a dogmatic formula. This always appears where two series of counter-arguments having the same form are interfering with each other. The intersection of the two lines of logic gives the centre where the antinomy is crystalized and represents its differential diagnosis from nonsense. The antinomic specificity of human thinking has been frequently embodied in human spirituality, mainly at a time of transition from a cultural paradigm to another. On this line, the difference noted by Lucian Blaga between the theory of relativity, which he sees more as the peak of classical physics, and the quantum theory, which truly revolutionises the spirit, is highly significant. Einstein, says the Romanian philosopher, settled, however, the contradiction raised by Michelson's experiment, by asymetrically changing the anatomy of the matter and building the time-space relation which admits the constant speed of light. It cannot be imagined in the factual world, but it can be understood in its theoretical build-up which saves the existing logic. A similar approach is taken to build the non-Euclidian geometries. However, in the quantum theory, because of the simultaneity of the continuous and the discontinuous elements, the complementarity is completely incomprehensible with the logic of identity. All the attempts to explain the undulatory and corpuscular ways as two aspects of an unknown third reality did not work out the expected asymmetry.

The antinomy was theoretically used, as Blaga noticed, by Christian dogma (see, for example, the Eucharistic trans-substantiality). The style of this dogma is morphologically similar to the style of the scientific discoveries, Blaga does not deem a transfigured antinomy to signal a deadlock by the scientific versatility of this way of thinking, but rather a mutational switch onto a new path of rationality. (A.B.)

The unconscious: is an ample psychic reality, with its own structures, dynamics, and initiatives: we imagine the unconscious feature a substantial core organized according to immanent laws. The unconscious is not a mere 'chaos' of a 'conscious' nature. We must insist to imagine the unconscious as a highly complex psychic reality, with sovereign functions, having an inner order and equilibrium, thanks to which it becomes a self-sufficient factor to a larger extent than 'conscience'. It might be far-fetched to say that the unconscious is a cosmos; it is however something that looks much like a cosmos. Were we allowed to make an adjective from the noun 'cosmos', such as 'chaotic' was formed from the noun 'chaos', we would attach the unconscious an epithet, respectively. The unconscious has a 'cosmiotic' nature, not a 'chaotic' one. 'Cosmiotic is any reality of a profound inner complexity, of a large diversity of elements and structures, organized according to an immanent order, rounded in its meanings, having the equilibrium centre within itself, that is, it is self-sufficient. In keeping with the sense we attach to this term, we shall take the chance to state that the unconscious, as a psychic reality, possesses a more 'cosmiotic' character than consciousness. It is the first time when term cosmiotic is used, more than that, in relation to the unconscious, which may have been seen only as the stubborn denial of the cosmic order.

Bibliography

1. Blaga's Philosophical Works

As he announced in his 'Philosophical Self-Presentation', Blaga began to organise his work into Trilogies, except for the first three books. To the first trilogy, his daughter added two other volumes, thus making it into a pentology, and she also put together the final trilogy. There have also been posthumously published works which do not fit into the trilogies. Where applicable, the following lists the works in trilogies, with dates of the first publication of each book and of their republication as trilogies, along with the titles of the essays or chapters in each.

Culture and Cognition (1922)
The Philosophy of Style (1924)
The Original Phenomenon (1925)

The Trilogy of Knowledge (1943)

On Philosophical Consciousness (1947)
Introductory considerations; Autonomy of philosophy and metaphysical creation; Philosophy and common sense; Philosophy, science, experience; Philosophical and scientific problems; Philosophy and method; Visionary aspects of philosophy; On scientism; Myth and magic in philosophy; The transcendental accent; The motive of philosophy; Thought and system; Efficiency; Philosophy and style; Philosophy and art; On philosophical consciousness.

The Dogmatic Aeon (1931)
Introductory considerations; Historical aspects of dogma; Transfigured antimony; Metaphysical paradoxes; Contradictions in science and dogma; Prelogical thought and dogma; Enstatic and Ecstatic intellect; Dogma and the transcendent; Dogma and experience; Dogmatism and the theory of knowledge; The perspectives of minus-knowledge; The dogmatic aeon.

Luciferian Knowledge (1933)
Introduction; Paradisaic and Luciferian knowledge; The crisis of objects; Qualitative variation of mysteries; The 'phanic' and the cryptic; The interior tension of problems in general; The double functions of categories; Theoretical ideas; The 'phanic' material; Problems and theories; Directed observation; Levels of revelation; Permanentised mysteries; Minus-knowledge; Transcendent variants and the typology of mysteries; On explanation; Cryptic un-

knowns and 'hiatus' unknowns; The inconvertibility of irrationals; Closure.

Transcendental Censorship (1937)

Introduction; Transcendental censorship; Dissimulating revelations; Ontology of censorship; Integration with mystery; The place of reasons; The level of creations and the apology of mysteries; Knowledge as a 'phenomenon' and knowledge as a 'non-phenomenon'; Metaphysical forms of knowledge; Spirit and realisation; The Great Anonym; Closure.

Experiment and the Mathematical Spirit (1969)

Galilean-Newtonian science and the premises of history; Logicians and the experimental method; Methods, methodological couplings, supermethod; Scientific intuition and Positivist errors; The mathematization of the methods of scientific investigation and philosophical panmathematicism; Modes of rationalisation; Common sense and scientific knowledge; Experiment and theory; The two lines of development and experiments; Experiment in the perspective of what it licences and its fruitfulness; Precise and statistical laws.

The Trilogy of Culture (1944)

Horizon and Style (1936)

The phenomenon of style and methodology; The other world; On personance; Culture and space; Between landscape and the unconscious horizon; Temporal horizons; The theory of doublings; The axiological accent; Anabasic and catabasic attitudes; Formative aspirations; The stylistic matrix.

The Mioritic Space (1936)

The Mioritic space; Bipolar spirituality; The descending transcendent; The Sophianic perspective; On assimilation; The picturesque and revelation; Spirit and ornamentation; On longing; Intermezzo; Evolution and involution; Modelling and catalytic influences; Romanian apriorism.

The Genesis of Metaphor and the Meaning of Culture (1937)

Minor and major cultures; The genesis of metaphor; On myths; Fundamental aspects of cultural creations; Abyssal categories; Fundamental concepts in the science of art; Cosmos and cosmoid; *Sub specie* style; The metaphysical meaning of culture; The impasses of creative destiny; The uniqueness of man.

The Trilogy of Value (1946)

Science and Creation (1942)

Clarifications; The circle of Saros and the Babylonian spirit; Variations on an atomist theme; The other theme in antiquity and modern times; Models of Greek scientific thought (ideas of spheres, qualitative mathematicism, volumes and fullness, resistance to the idea of infinity, resistance to the idea of becoming);

Plato's idea of science; Aristotle's idea of science; The Arabic scientific spirit; The Indian scientific spirit; The great European anticipation; The principle of inertia and its implications; The Baroque involution; Romantic categories; The physics of sensation; Constructivism; The guiding functions of abyssal categories; The adjustment of style to ideas and observations; On the stylistic field; Some problems of the theory of knowledge (categorial concepts—subjective or objective?; categorial concepts—general or not?); The two types of knowledge.

Magical Thought and Religion

On Magical Thought (1941)

Myth and magic; Points of view (Group I, II, III, IV); The co-ordinates of the creative spirit; Myth and co-ordinates; Magic and co-ordinates; The salt of any culture; The magical charge; Experience and superstition; The autonomy of magic; The cognitive function of the idea of magic; Other functions; The polyvalency of the idea of magic.

Religion and Spirit (1942)

Introduction; From Indra to Nirvana; The Tao; Cosmic health; Measure and ecstasy; The generalised miracle; Uncreated light; The birth of the logos; The mystical state and belief; earthquake-belief; The religion of sacred thrill; The definition of religion; The Sacred; Certitude and superconsciousness.

Art and Values (1939)

The theoretical structure; The amphibianism of consciousness; On art in general; Aesthetic satisfaction from art; The autonomy of art; The law of non-transponsibility; Aesthetics of intropathy and of life-experience; Polar values; Vicarious values; Abyssal categories as canalising factors; Tertiary values; Art and genres; The universal man; Accessory values; Crystal, organism, cosmoid; The ethnic, art and mythology; The metaphysics of values.

The Cosmological Trilogy (1980-8)

The Divine Differentials 1940)

Preface; Models of genesis; The Great Anonym, the generator; The maximal limitation of divine possibilities; The divine differentials; Individuals, types, sources; Ontological modes; Finality and parafinality; The theory of formative unity; A metaphysical explanation of evolution; Between the Anonymous Source and individuation; The pluralism of individuation; The organising of space; On history; Another datum: the uniqueness of man; Measure and advantage; Finalistic indetermination; The paradoxes of concepts.

Anthropological Aspects (1947-8)

Introductory remarks; Lamarck and the idea of transformism; Darwin and natural selection; The theory of selection; Specialisation and the level of organisation; Anthropogenesis and the problems it presents; Problems of biological primitivism, a new explanation; Instinct, intelligence, genius; Archetypes and stylistic factors; Closing remarks; Diagrams.

Historical Existence (1959)

On historiography; The historical phenomenon; The permanence of prehistory; Organism and society; Stylistic fields; Styles and dialectic; The duration of stylistic factors; Stylistic interference; Ideas of progress in history; Phenomena, knowledge, zones of censorship; Oswald Spengler and the philosophy of history; The metaphysics of history.

Romanian Thought in Transylvania in the 18th Century (1966)

Horizons and Stages (1968)

Sources (essays, lectures, articles) (1972)

Philosophical Endeavours (1977)

2. Translations of Blaga's Works

The Great Transition. Trans. Roy MacGregor-Hastie. Preface by Ion Dodu Balan. Bucharest: Ed. Eminescu, 1975.

Complete Poetical Works of Lucian Blaga, Trans. Brenda Walker, Iasi, RO, Oxford, Portland, OR: Center for Romanian Studies, 2001.

Orizzonte e stile. Ed. Antonio Banfi. Translation in Italian by M. Popescu, E. Coseriu, Milan: Ed. Minuziano, 1946.

Poesie 1919-1943. Transl. in Italian, ed. with preface by Rosa del Conte. Rome: Lerici Editore, 1971.

En el gran correr. Transl. in Spanish by Darie Novaceanu, Edgar Papu, ed. Bucharest: Ed. Minerva, 1972.

Aura ja huilu. Transl. in Finnish by Marti Larno. Helsinki: Oy Soumen Jirja, 1945.

Sinr dunyasi ve bir piyes. Transl. in Turkish by Enver Esenkova. Istanbul: Matbaacilik, 1958.

Magikus virradat. Transl. in Hungarian by Samuel Domokos. Budapest: Ed. Europa, 1965.

Nebeski dodir. Transl. in Serbian by Adam Puslojic. Belgrade: Ed. Prosveta, 1975.

Ausgewählte Gedichte. Transl. in Germanby Oskar Pastior. Bucharest: Ed. Tineretului, 1967.

Zum Wesen der rumänischen Volksseele. Transl. in Germanby Julius Draser. Introduction by Dumitru Ghișe. Mircea Flonta, editor. Bucharest: Ed. Minerva, 1967.

L'Eon dogmatique. Transl. in French by Georges Piscoci-Danesco et collab. Paris: Librairie Roumaine Antitotalitaire, 1988.

L'Éloge du village roumain. Transl. in French by Georges Piscoci-Danesco et collab. Paris: Librairie Roumaine Antitotalitaire, 1989.

L'Étoile la plus triste. Transl. in French by Sanda Stolojan. Paris: de, 1992.

L'Être historique. Transl. in French by Georges Piscoci-Danesco et collab. Paris: Librairie Roumaine Antitotalitaire, 1993.

Les Différentielles divines. Transl. in French by Georges Piscoci-Danesco et collab. Paris: Librairie Roumaine Antitotalitaire, 1993.

Trilogie de la Connaissance. Transl. in French by Georges Piscoci-Danesco et collab. Paris: Librairie Roumaine Antitotalitaire, 1995.

Trilogie de la Culture. Transl. in French by Georges Piscoci-Danesco et collab. Paris: Librairie Roumaine Antitotalitaire, 1996.

Nebatrepte, anthology. 200 poems translated in Bulgarian by Ognean Stamboliev and Nikolai Zidarov. Sofia: Editura Narodna Kultura, 1985.

Poemele luminii. Poems and essays. Translation in Bulgarian and Preface by Ognean Stamboliev. Ruse: Editura Avangard Print, 2012.

3. Studies of Blaga's philosophy

Afloroaei, Ştefan. 'Antinomii ale intelectului ecstatic.' In *Lucian Blaga: Cunoaştere şi creaţie: culegere de studii*, edited by Dumitru Ghişe, Angela Botez, and Victor Botez. Bucharest: Cartea Românească, 1987.

Allen, R. T. 'Why Read Blaga's Philosophy?' *Revue Roumaine de Philosophie*, nos. 1-2 (2005): 11-14.

― 'Prolegomena to the Philosophy of Culture: R. G. Collingwood and Lucian Blaga.' *Revue Roumaine de Philosophie*, nos. 1-2 (2006): 3-13.

― Review of Michael S. Jones. *The Metaphysics of Religion: Lucian Blaga and Contemporary Religion*. Madison and Teaneck, N.J.: Fairleigh Dickinson UP, 2006. In *Appraisal*, vol. 6, no. 4 (2007): 33-5. Translation. Şerban, Henrieta A., in *Revista de filosofie*, nos.5-6 (2007): 755-6.

Antonesei, Liviu. 'Repere pentru o filosofie a culturii.' In *Lucian Blaga: Cunoaştere şi creaţie*, edited by Dumitru Ghişe, Angela Botez, and Victor Botez. Bucharest: Cartea Românească, 1987.

Bălu, Ion. *Lucian Blaga*. Bucharest: Editura Albatros, 1986.

― *Viata lui Lucian Blaga.* Bucharest: Editura Libra, 1995.

Bancilă, Vasile. *Lucian Blaga: Energie romaneasca*. Timişoara, Romania: Editura Marineasa, 1995.ş

Banf, Antonio, ed. *Orizzonte e stile*. Milano: Minuziano Editore, 1946; *Filosofia dell' Arte*, Editori Riuniti, Rome.

Bazin, Thomas, Raoul Marin, and Georges Piscoci-Danesco, trans. *Les Differentielles divines*. Paris: Librairie du Savoir, 1990.

Blaga, Dorli, ed. *Lucian Blaga: Opere*. Vols 7-11. Bucharest: Editura Minerva, 1980-87.

― *Lucian Blaga: Opere*. Bucharest: Editura Humanitas, 1992-2006.

Boboc, Alexandru. *'Blaga, Nietzsche şi Spengler.* In *Dimensiunea metafizică a operei lui Lucian Blaga*, edited by Angela Botez, 276-80. Bucharest: Editura Ştiinţifică, 1996.

Borcea, M., and V. Soran. 'The Romanian Philosopher Lucian Blaga on the General Problems of Biology.' *Noesis* 17 (1991): 125-36.

Borcilă, Mircea. *Eonul Blaga: Intaiul veac.* Bucharest: Editura Albatros, 1997.

Botez, Angela. 'Campul stilistic și evolutia stiintei.' In *Dimensiunea metafizică a operei lui Lucian Blaga,* edited by Angela Botez, 261—66. Bucharest: Editura Științifică, 1996.

'La Catégorie Essentielle de la Spatialité dans la Philosophie de Lucian Blaga.' *Revue roumaine de philosophie et logique* 39 (1995): 221-27.

'Comparativist and Valuational Reflections on Blaga's Philosophy.' *Revue roumaine de philosophie et logique* 40 (1996): 153-62.

'Lucian Blaga and the Complementary Spiritual Paradigm of the 20th Century.' *Revue roumaine de philosophie et logique* 37 (1993): 51-55.

'The Postmodern Antirepresentalionalism (Polanyi, Blaga, Rorty)', *Revue roumaine de philosophie et logique* 41 (1997): 59-70.

'Heidegger, Derrida, Blaga: Postmodernist Perspectives on Metaphysics' *Revue roumaine de philosophie*(2006): 13-19.

Arhitectura sistemului și conceptele integrative blagiene. Târgu Mureș: Editura Ardealul, 2006.

Botez, Angela, Dumitru Ghișe, and Victor Botez, eds. *Lucian Blaga: Cunoaștere și creație.* Bucharest: Cartea Românească, 1987.

Botez, Angela, ed. *Dimensiunea metafizică a operei lui Lucian Blaga.* Bucharest: Editura Științifică, 1996.

Botez, Angela, Victor Botez, and Mihai Popa, ed. *Lucian Blaga – Confluențe filosofice în perspectivă culturală.* Bucharest: Editura Academiei, 2007.

Botez, Victor. 'Blaga-omul, așa cum l-au cunoscut.' In *Lucian Blaga: Cunoaștere și creație,* edited by Dumitru Ghișe, Angela Botez, and Victor Botez. Bucharest: Cartea Românească, 1987.

Braga, Corin. Lucian Blaga. 'Geneza lumilor possible'. Iași: Institutul Eiropean, 1998.

Brucar, I. 'Filosoful Lucian Blaga.' *Gândirea* 13, no 8 (December 1934): 314-27.

'Lucian Blaga: 'Eonul Dogmatic.' *România Literară* 2, no. 56 (March 11, 1933): 1-2.

Busetto, Ricardo, and Marco Cugno, trans. *Trilogia della cultura: Lo spazio mioritico.* Alessandria, Italy: Editionni dell'Orso, 1994.

Cazan, Gh. Al. 'Lucian Blaga: Cunoaștere și creație; Culegere de studii.' In *Lucian Blaga: Cunoaștere și creație,* edited by Dumitru Ghișe, Angela Botez, and Victor Botez. Bucharest: Cartea Românească, 1987.

'Lucian Blaga sau Metafizica împotriva scientismului.' *Analele Universității din Bucuresti,* Seria Filosofie 40 (1991): 46-54.

Cernica, V. 'The Presence of the Speech about Man in Lucian Blaga's Philosophy.' *Revue roumaine de philosophie* nos.1-2 (2006): 47-63.

Cimpoi, M. 'Lucian Blaga, filosof al valorilor.' *Steaua* 44 (1993): 19-20.

Cioran, Emil. 'Lucian Blaga: 'Eonul Dogmatic.' *Revista de Filosofie* 16, nos. 3-4 (July-December 1931): 349-50.

Codoban, Aurel. 'Un Blaga ignorat: Filosoful religiei.' In *Eonul Blaga: Întâiul veac*, edited by Mircea Borcilă, 381-82. Bucharest: Editura Albatros, 1997.

— 'Blaga Eliade: Itinerare echivalente spre misterul unic al lumii.' In *Meridian Blaga*, edited by Irina Petras. Vol. 1. Cluj-Napoca, Romania: Casa Cărții de Știință, 2000.

— 'Matricea stilistica și structura semantica.' In *Dimensiunea metafizică a operei lui Lucian Blaga*, edited by Angela Botez, Bucharest: Editura Științifică, 1996, 298-302.

— *Sacru și Ontofanie: Pentru o nouă filosofie a religiilor.* Iași, Romania: Polirom, 1998.

Colțescu, Viorel. 'Lucian Blaga și morfologia spengleriană a culturii.' In *Lucian Blaga: Cunoaștere și creație; Culegere de studii*, edited by Dumitru Ghișe, Angela Botez, and Victor Botez, 357-79. Bucharest: Cartea Românească, 1987.

Comarnescu, Petru. 'Lucian Blaga: 'Cunoașterea luciferică'; Studiu filosofic.' *Revista de Filosofie* 18, no. 2 (April-June 1933): 254-57.

Constandache, G. G. 'Critique of the Unconscious: Kantian Influences in the Works of Lucian Blaga.' *Man and World* 30 (1997): 445-52.

— 'Lucian Blaga. Filosofie românească în context universal.' *Viața Românească* 90 (1995): 16-27.

del Conte, Rosa. 'Comunicarea eului profund prin iubire'. In *Dimensiunea metafizică a operei lui Lucian Blaga*, edited by Angela Botez, Bucharest: Editura Științifică, 1996.

Corteanu Loffredo, Nicoleta. *Profili di estetica europea. Lucian Blaga, Gaston Bachelard, Carl Gustav Jung.* Rome: Casa editrice Oreste Bayes, 1971.

Diaconu, Florica, and Marin Diaconu. *Dicționar de termeni filosofici ai lui Lucian Blaga.* Bucharest: Univers Enciclopedic, 2000.

Dima, Teodor. 'Ideea teorica: Fundament cognitiv general.' In *Eonul Blaga: Întâiul veac*, edited by Mircea Borcilă. Bucharest: Editura Albatros, 1997.

Drimba, Ovidiu. *Filosofia lui Blaga.* Bucharest: Cugetarea, 1944. Reprinted by the Excelsior-Multi Press, 1995.

Eliade, Mircea. 'Convorbiri cu Lucian Blaga.' In *Lucian Blaga: Cunoaștere și creație; Culegere de studii*, edited by Dumitru Ghișe, Angela Botez, and Victor Botez. Bucharest: Cartea Românească, 1987.

— 'Lucian Blaga și sensul culturii.' *Revista Fundațiilor Regale* 5, no. 1 (January- March 1938): 162-66.

'Rumanian Philosophy.' In *Encyclopedia of Philosophy*, edited by Paul Edwards. New York: Macmillan and the Free Press, 1967.

Faggin, Giuseppe. 'L'estetica stilistica di Lucian Blaga.' *Rivista di Istoria e di Filosofia*, 2, no. 2 (April-June 1947).

Flonta, Mircea. 'Analiza culturală a cunoașterii positive.' In *Dimensiunea metafizică a operei lui Lucian Blaga*, edited by Angela Botez, 257-60. Bucharest: Editura Științifică, 1996.

'Blaga, Lucian.' In *Routledge Encyclopedia of Philosophy Online*, edited by E. Craig. London: Routledge, 2004, http://www.rep.routledge.com/article/N109 (accessed January 3, 2006).

Cum recunoaștem pasărea Minervei? Reflecții asupra percepției filosofice în cultura românească. Bucharest: Editura Fundației Culturale Române, 1998.

'În ce sens are cunoașterea științifică o istorie?' In *Cunoaștere și acțiune*, edited by Andrei Marga. Cluj-Napoca, Romania: Editura Dacia, n.d.

'Istoria științei și analiza culturală a cunoașterii.' In *Lucian Blaga: Cunoaștere și creație*, edited by Dumitru Ghișe, Angela Botez, and Victor Botez. Bucharest: Cartea Românească, 1987.

'Metafizica cunoașterii și sistem metafizic la Lucian Blaga.' *Revista de Filosofie* 42 (1995): 507-19. Reprinted in vol. I of *Meridian Blaga*, edited by Irina Petraș. Cluj- Napoca, Romania: Casa Cărții de Știință, 2000.

'Unitatea sistematică a filosofiei lui Lucian Blaga.' In *Meridian Blaga*, edited by Irina Petraș. Vol. 2. Cluj-Napoca, Romania: Casa Cărții de Știință , 2002., ed. *Zum Wesen der rumanischen Volkseele*. Bucharest: Editura Minerva, 1982.

Frunză, Sandu. 'Aspecte ale polemicii Blaga-Stăniloae în jurul definirii religiei.' Paper presented at the Twelfth International Lucian Blaga Festival, Cluj-Napoca, Romania, May 13, 2002.

Gană, George. *Opera literară a lui Lucian Blaga*, series Universitas. Bucharest: Editura Minerva, 1976.,

ed. *Lucian Blaga – Opere complete*. Bucharest: Editura Minerva, 1982-83.

Gavriliu, Leonard. *Inconștientul în viziunea lui Lucian Blaga: Preludii la o Noologie Abisală*. Bucharest: Editura IRI, 1997.

Gheorghe, I. 'Paul Valery et Lucian Blaga face au mystere.' *Bulletin des Etudes Valeryennes Montpellier* 31 (1982): 27-47.

Ghișe, Dumitru, Angela Botez and Victor Botez., eds. *Lucian Blaga: Cunoaștere și creație: Culegere de studii*. Bucharest: Cartea Românească, 1987.

Gogoneață, Nicolae. 'Problema cunoașterii la Blaga.' *Revista de filosofie* 14, no. 6 (June 15, 1967): 625-35.

Gruia, Bazil. *Blaga inedit: amintiri și documente*. Cluj-Napoca, Romania: Editura Dacia, 1974.

Blaga inedit. Efigii documentare. 2 vols. Cluj-Napoca, Romania: Editura Dacia,1981.

Haranguș, Cornel. 'Blaga: Filosof al istoriei.' In *Meridian Blaga*, edited by Irina Petraș. Vol. 1. Cluj-Napoca, Romania: Casa Cărții de Știință, 2000.

'Metafizica lui Blaga: Procedee de elaborare.' *Caietele Lucian Blaga* 11 (May 2001), 16-22.

Hitchins, Keith. Introduction to *Complete Poetical Works of Lucian Blaga*, translated by Brenda Walker, 23-48. Iași, Romania, Oxford, UK, Portland, OR: Center for Romanian Studies, 2001.

Ionescu, Petru. P. 'Adevăr și cunoaștere.' *Gândirea* 22, no. 2 (February 1943): 85-94.

'Lucian Blaga: Despre gândirea magică.' *Gândirea* 20, no. 7 (September 1941): 388-90.

Isac, Dumitru. 'Diferențialele Divine: Considerații critice.' *Revista de Filosofie* 25, no. 2 (April-June 1940): 193-99.

'Lucian Blaga și Marele Anonim.' *Symposion* 3, no. 1 (June 1943): 25-48.

'Lucian Blaga, teoretician al cunoașterii.' *Freamătul școalei* 4, nos. 5-6 (May-June 1938): 199-231.

Itu, Mircea. *Indianismul lui Blaga*, Brașov, Romania: Editura Orientul Latin, 1996.

Jones, Michael S. 'Blaga's Philosophy of Culture: More than a Spenglerian Adaptation.' *Studia Universitatis Babes-Bolyai, Seria Philosophia*, 48, nos. 1-22 (2003).

The Metaphysics of Religion: Lucian Blaga and Contemporary Philosophy. NJ: Fairleigh Dickinson, 2006.

'Lucian Blaga on the Existence of God'. In *Meridian Blaga*, edited by Irina Petraș. Vol. 2. Cluj-Napoca, Romania: Casa Cărții de Știință, 2008.

Macoviciuc, V. '"Stylistic Matrix". Interpretative Hypotheses.' *Revue roumaine de philosophie* nos. 1-2 (2006): 29-33.

Marga, Andrei. *Cunoaștere și acțiune. Profiluri de gânditori români.* Cluj-Napoca, Romania: Dacia, 1986.

Mare, Călina, *Preface*, ed. *Experimentul și spiritul matematic.* Bucharest: Editura Științifică, 1969.

Marin, Jessie, and Raoul Marin, eds. *L'Eloge du village roumain.* Paris: Librairie du Savoir, 1989.

Marin, Jessie, Raoul Marin, Mariana Danesco, and Georges Piscoci-Danesco, trans. *L'Eon dogmatique. L'Age d'Homme.* Lausanne: Editions l'Age d'Home, 1988.

Marin, Raoul, and Georges Pișcoci-Dănescu, trans. *La trilogie de la connaissance.* Paris: Librairie du Savoir, 1992.

Maxim, Ion. 'Lucian Blaga și conștiința filosofică.' *Viața Românească* 27, no. 3 (March 1974): 33-45.

Micu, Dumitru. 'Lucian Blaga: Un sistem filosofic axat pe cultură.' In *Dimensiunea metafizică a operei lui Lucian Blaga*, edited by Angela Botez. Bucharest: Editura Științifică, 1996, 231-38.

Mihu, Achim. *Dimensiunea metafizică a operei lui Lucian Blaga: Antologie de texte din și despre opera filosofică*. Ed. Angela Botez. Bucharest: Editura Științifică, 1996.

    Lucian Blaga: Miorița cultă a spiritualității românești. Bucharest: Editura Viitorul Românesc, 1995.

    'Lucian Blaga și gnosticismul.' *Steaua* 43 (1992): 60-61.

Mocanu, Titus. 'Blaga: Filosof al culturii.' *România literară* 3, no. 20 (May 14, 1970): 23.

Munteanu, Bazil. 'Lucian Blaga: Metafizician al misterului și filosof al culturii.' In *Dimensiunea metafizică a operei lui Lucian Blaga*, edited by Angela Botez. Bucharest: Editura Științifică, 1996, 204-11.

    'Lucian Blaga, Metaphysician of Mystery and Philosopher of Culture.' *Revue roumaine de philosophie et logique*, 39 (1995): 43-46.

Muscă, Vasile. *Filosofia ideii naționale la Lucian Blaga și D. D. Roșca*. Cluj-Napoca, Romania: Biblioteca Apostrof, 1996.

    'Specificul creației culturale românești în câmpul filosofiei.' In *Lucian Blaga: Cunoaștere și creație*, edited by Dumitru Ghișe, Angela Botez, and Victor Botez. Bucharest: Cartea Românească, 1987.

Muthu, Mircea. *Lucian Blaga: Dimensiuni răsăritene*. Pitești, Brașov, and Cluj-Napoca, Romania: Editura Paralela 45, 2000.

    'Prospecțiuni morfologice: L. Blaga și O. Spengler.' In *Lucian Blaga: Dimensiuni răsăritene*. Pitești, Brașov, and Cluj-Napoca, Romania: Editura Paralela 45, 2000.

Noica, Constantin. 'Filosofia d-lui Lucian Blaga după "Trilogia Culturii."' *Revista Fundațiilor Regale* 5, no. 2 (February 1, 1938): 388-404.

    'Un filosof original: Lucian Blaga.' *Revista Fundațiilor Regale* 1, no. 12 (December 1, 1934): 687-91.

    'Viziunea metafizică a lui Lucian Blaga și veacul al XX-lea.' In *Dimensiunea metafizică a operei lui Lucian Blaga*, edited by Angela Botez, 212— 17. Bucharest: Editura Științifică, 1996.

Nemoianu, Virgil. 'Mihai Sora and the Traditions of Romanian Philosophy.' *Review of Metaphysics* 43 (March 1990): 591-605.

    A Theory of the Secondary: Literature, Progress, and Reaction. Baltimore, MD: Johns Hopkins University Press, 1989.

Papu, Edgar. 'Lucian Blaga: "Geneza metaforei și sensul culturii."' *Revista de Filosofie* 22, no. 4 (October-December 1937): 464-66.

    'Lucian Blaga: "Orizont și stil."' *Revista de Filosofie* 21, no. 1 (January-March 1936): 84-86. 'Spațiul Mioritic.' *Revista de Filosofie* 21, no. 3 (July-September 1936): 306-8.

Pârvu, I. 'Despre problema individuației în metafizica lui Lucian Blaga.' *In Lucian Blaga. Confluențe filosofice în perspectivă culturală*, 330-335. Bucharest: Editura Academiei Române, 2007.

Petraș, Irina, ed. *Meridian Blaga*. 3 vols. Cluj-Napoca, Romania: Casa Cărții de Știință, 2000-2003.

Petre, Cipriana. 'Mioritic Space.' In *Ten Steps Closer to Romania*. Bucharest: Romanian Cultural Foundation Publishing House, 1999.

Petreu, Marta. 'De la Dumnezeul cel bun la Dumnezeul cel rău.' In *Meridian Blaga*, edited by Irina Petraș. Vol. 1. Cluj-Napoca, Romania: Casa Cărții de Știință, 2002.

Petru, Cristian. 'Cunoaștere și existență creatoare.' In *Lucian Blaga: Cunoaștere și creație*, edited by Dumitru Ghișe, Angela Botez, and Victor Botez. Bucharest: Cartea Românească, 1987.

Petru, Ioan. 'Matricea kantiană a filosofiei lui Blaga.' *Revista de Filosofie* 44 (1997): 213-21.

Pop, Traian. *Introducere in filosofia lui Lucian Blaga*. Cluj-Napoca, Romania: Editura Dacia, 2001.

Popa, Grigore. 'Artă și Valoare.' *Pagini Literare* 6, nos. 7-12 (July-December 1939): 193-201.

'Despre "Censura Transcendentă."' *Pagini Literare* 1, nos. 3-4 (July-August 1934): 129-45.

'Lucian Blaga ca filosof al culturii.' *Pagini Literare* 3, no. 2 (February 15, 1936): 113-19.

Popescu, Ion Mihail. *O perspectivă românească asupra Teoriei Culturii* și *Valorilor. Bazele TeorieiCulturii* și *Valorilor în sistemul lui Lucian Blaga*. Bucharest: Editura Eminescu, 1980.

Teoria culturii și *valorilor în filosofia lui Lucian Blaga*. Bucharest: Universitatea București, 1974.

Roșca, D. D. 'Despre o istorie a inteligenței (Încercare de lărgire a noțiunii de "rațional").' *Școala Românească* 7-8 (July-August 1931): 89-113. Reprinted in *Linii și Figuri*. Sibiu, Romania: Editura 'Țara,' 1943; and also in *Studii Eseuri Filosofice*. Bucharest: Editura Științifică, 1970.

Schrag, Calvin Otto. 'Filosofia la sfârșitul secolului al XX-lea cu un comentariu despre Lucian Blaga.' In *Dimensiunea metafizică a operei lui Lucian Blaga*, edited by Angela Botez. Bucharest: Editura Științifică, 1996, 306-313.

Șerban, Henrieta A., and Eric Gilder. 'Blaga and Rorty. The Historical Being and the Ironism.' *Revue roumanine de philosophie*, nos. 1-2 (2006): 19-29.

Stahl, H. H. 'Filozofarea despre filozofia poporului român.' *Sociologie Românească* 3, nos. 4-6 (April-June 1938): 104-19.

'Teoria abisală a d-lui Lucian Blaga.' *Sociologie Românească* 3, no.s 1-3, (January-March 1938): 10-18.

Stăniloae, Dumitru. *Poziția d-lui Lucian Blaga față de Creștinism și Ortodoxie.* Sibiu, Romania: Tiparul Tipografiei Arhidicezane, 1942. Reprinted with notes by Mihai-Petru Georgescu. Bucharest: Editura Paideia, 1993.

Tănase, Alexandra. *Lucian Blaga: Filosoful poet, poetul filosof.* Bucharest: Cartea Românească, 1977.

Vaida, Mircea. *Pe urmele lui Lucian Blaga.* Bucharest: Sport-Turism, 1982.

Vatamaniuc, D. *Lucian Blaga, 1895—1961: Biobibliografie.* Bucharest: Editura Științifică și Enciclopedică, 1977.

Vlăduțescu, Gheorghe. 'Începuturile filosofice ale lui Lucian Blaga.' *Revista de Filozofie* 15, no. 1 (January 1968): 73-81.

Vlăduțescu, Gheorghe. 'Independenții. Lucian Blaga.' *Neconvențional despre filosofia românească.* Bucharest: Editura Paidea, 2002.

Vulcănescu, Mircea. 'Un sistem: în jurul filosofiei lui Blaga.' *Criterion* 1, no. 4 (December 15, 1934): 3.

Wald, Henri. 'Un logician contemporan.' *Revista Fundațiilor Regale* 13, no. 9 (September 1946): 84-95.

'Metaforă și mit.' *Viața Românească* 26, no. 11 (November 1973): 84-90.Zamfirescu, Ion. *Spiritualități românești.* Bucharest: Monitorul Oficial 51, Imprimeriile Statului, 1941.

Zamfirescu, Vasile Dem. 'Filosofia culturii și psihoanaliza la Lucian Blaga.' In *Dimensiunea metafizică a operei lui Lucian Blaga,* edited by Angela Botez. Bucharest: Editura Științifică, 1996, 271-75.

Zevedei, Barbu. 'Metafizicul ca funcțiune integrală a spiritului.' *Saeculum* 1, no. 1 (January-February 1943): 50-76.

4. Entries in encyclopedias

Der Grosse Brockhaus. Wiesbaden: Brokhaus, 1967.

Dictionnaire encyclopédique Quillet. Paris: Quillet, 1968.

Dictionnaire des oeuvres. Paris: Presses Universitaire de France, 1992.

Enciclopedia Italiana di Scienze, Lettere et Arti. Roma: Istituto della Enciclopedia Italiana, 1950.

Encyclopaedia Britannica. Vol. 19. Cambridge: New York University Press, 1911.

Edwards, Paul ed. *The Encyclopedia of Philosophy.* London, New York: Macmillan and Free Press, 1967.

Grand Larousse encyclopédique in ten volumes.Paris: Librairie Larousse, 1960.

Grande dizionario enciclopedico. Founded by Pietro Fedele. Torino: UTET, 1955.

Prokhorov, A. M. ed. *Great Soviet Encyclopedia.* 31 volumes, three volumes of indexes. New York: Macmillan, London: Collier Macmillan, 1974-83.

Routledge Encyclopedia of Philosophy Online, edited by E. Craig. London: Routledge, 2004, http://www.rep.routledge.com/article/N109

Index

A

Alexander, the Great, 38
Allen, R.T., 6, 167
Alsberg, P., 24
Arhipenko, 94
Aristotelian, 56, 154
Aristotle, 33, 56, 57, 92, 154, 165

B

Bach, J.S., 129, 130
Banfi, A., 11, 166
Barbu, I., ix, 9
Barlach, E., 94
Berdiaev, N., 2, 13, 24, 42, 43
Bergson, H., 2, 8, 94
Blaga, D., 2
Bose, J.G., 93
Brâncuși, C., 9, 94
Bunge, M., 5

C

Carol II, 2
Cassirer, E., 2, 8
Chomsky, N., 5
Collingwood, R.G., 5
Conta, V., 3
Conte, R. del, 2
Critchley, S., 13, 14, 25

D

Darwin, C., 165
Descartes, R., 18, 19, 87
Driesch, H., 74, 75
Dvorak, M., 15, 25, 110

E

Einstein, A., 71, 79, 94, 160
Emerson, R.W., 7

F

Fichte, J.G., 94
Florian, M., 3
Foucault, F., 7
Freud, S., 2, 8, 157
Frobenius, L., 15, 25, 32, 33, 110, 132, 157

G

Gandhara, 120
Gehlen, A., 8, 24
Gilder, E., 13, 24
Goethe, J.W., 2, 9, 112, 113, 128

H

Hebbel, C.F., 112, 128
Hegel, G.W.F., 9, 94
Hegelian, 19
Heidegger, M., 2, 7, 18, 150
Heisenberg, W., 152
Heraclitus, 69, 142
Hölderlin, F., 32
Husserl, E., 2

I

Indra, 165

J

Jones, M., ix, 11, 167
Jung, C., 2, 10

K

Kant, I., 2, 6, 7, 19, 29, 30, 33, 71, 78, 83, 85, 87, 90, 117, 149, 150, 153, 155, 157
Kantian, 5, 47, 85, 149, 158
Kantianism, 9

Keyserling, H.A., 15, 24, 39, 42, 110
Koyré, A., 5
Kuhn, T., 5, 17, 71, 83, 159

L

Lamarck, J.-B., 165
Laszlo, E., 5
Leibniz, G., 52, 58, 87, 94, 108
Leonardo, da Vinci, 87, 111, 112
Lessing, G.E., 2
Lévy-Bruhl, L., 7
Locke, J., 6
Lupasco, S., 3, 5

M

Mach, E., 94
MacIntyre, A., 16
Manet, E., 94
Mayer, R., 94
Merleau-Ponty, M., 18, 20
Michelson, A.A., 160
Mircea, 166
Munteanu, B., 2

N

Nagarjuna, 126
Newton, I., 29, 71, 79, 87, 155, 159
Nietzsche, F., 2, 8, 32, 102, 110
Noica, C., 3
Nozick, R., 16

P

Parmenides, 69
Parvati, 121
Petrovici, I., 2
Planck, M., 152
Plato, 109, 165
Platonic, 29, 55, 58, 94, 95, 128
Platonism, 51, 128
Plotinus, 51
Poe, E.A., 112

Polanyi, M., 5, 6, 7, 18, 24, 168
Popper, K., 19
Praxiteles, 109
Prigogine, I., 5
Ptolemy, 93

R

Ramsey, E., ix, 7, 24
Rembrandt, 108, 121
Rickert, H., 95
Riegl, A., 15, 25, 33, 110, 132, 133, 150
Rorty, R., 5, 7, 13, 14, 24, 25
Roşca, D.D., 3

S

Sankara, 124
Schlegel, A.W. and F., 32
Schrag, C.O., ix, 7
Serban, H., x, 13, 24
Simmel, G., 15, 25, 32, 110
Siva, 121
Spengler, O., 2, 13, 15, 24, 32, 33, 42, 110, 132, 157, 166
Spinoza, B., 69
Steiner, R., 39

T

Taylor, C., 16
Thorn, R., 5
Thorndike, E.L., 19
Tuculescu, I. ,, 9

V

Valéry, P., 112

W

Windelband, W., 95
Wölfflin, H., 15, 25, 33
Worringer, W., 15, 25, 33, 110, 132
Wundt, W., 72

CPSIA information can be obtained
at www.ICGtesting.com
Printed in the USA
BVHW041141280720
584856BV00005B/19/J